MW01532641

𝕻rimitibe Christianity
REVIVED
IN THE
Faith & Practice
Of the PEOPLE called
QUAKERS.

Written, in Testimony of the present Dispensation of God, through Them, to the World: that Prejudices may be removed, the Simple informed, the Well-enclined Encouraged, and the Truth and its Innocent Friends, Rightly Represented.

By *William Penn*

This People have I formed for my self: They shall shew forth my Praise, Isaiah 43:21

Translated into Modern English by
Paul Buckley

Inner Light Books
San Francisco, California

Cover and book design: Paul Buckley

Back cover photograph: Charles Moore

Editor: Charles Martin

Copy editor: Kathy McKay

Published by Inner Light Books, San Francisco, California

www.innerlightbooks.com

editor@innerlightbooks.com

Library of Congress Control Number: 2018931361

ISBN 978–0-9998332–0-9 (hardcover)

ISBN 978–0-9998332–1-6 (paperback)

Contents

Acknowledgments   ix

Translator's Preface   xi

Truth, Revelation, and Apostasy   xii
The Bible   xiii
The Translation   xiv

An Epistle to the Reader   1

Chapter 1   5

Friends' Fundamental Principle   5
The Nature of This Principle   5
The Names Given This Principle   5
Faith and Practice, Ministry and Worship   6

Chapter 2   9

Evidence in Scripture   9
The Divinity of the Light   9
All Things Created by the Word   10
What the Light Has to Do with Salvation   10

Chapter 3   11

How This Scripture Is Distorted   11
The Claim That It Is a Natural Light   11
The Claim That Not All Are Enlightened   12
The Claim That It Is the Doctrine and the Example of
    Christ's Life That Enlightens   12

Chapter 4   **15**

The Power of the Inward Light to Grant Discernment   15

The Light Reveals God   16

The Light Gives Life to the Soul   17

The Light Is the Apostolic Message   17

An Objection About Two Lights Answered   18

Natural and Spiritual Light: There Are neither Two
    Darknesses nor Two Lights   18

The Objection Is Fully Answered by the Apostle John   20

Chapter 5   **23**

The Light Is the Same as the Spirit of God   23

The Properties of the Light and the Spirit Compared   24

The Light and the Spirit Flow from the Same Source   25

An Objection Answered   25

The Differences in Appearance or Action   26

Chapter 6   **29**

Although All Are Enlightened, Not All Are Good   29

Gospel Truths Were Known Before Christ   30

The Gentiles Had the Same Light But without the Same
    Advantages   32

Chapter 7   **35**

The Various Dispensations of God   35

Truth Is the Same in All Forms   36

Why Idolatry Abounds   36

The Quakers' Testimony Is the Best Antidote:
    Walking by a Divine Principle   37

The Purpose of All God's Manifestations:
    That Humanity Might Be God's Image and Delight   38

Contents

Chapter 8   **41**

Satisfaction and Justification according to the Scriptures   41

Notions We Cannot Believe   42

Christ, a Sacrifice and a Mediator   43

The Two Parts of Justification: From the Guilt of Sin
and from Sin's Power and Pollution   44

Exhortation to the Reader   45

Chapter 9   **47**

Belief in Christ and in His Work, Both in His Doings
and in His Sufferings   47

Our Belief in and Testimony of Christ's Inward and
Spiritual Appearance in the Soul   48

It Is Impossible to Be Saved by Christ While Rejecting
His Work and Power within Us   48

The Dispensation of Grace: Its Nature and Extent   49

Acknowledgment of the Death and Sufferings of Christ   50

Our Adversaries' Unreasonableness   52

Chapter 10   **55**

The True Worship of God   55

True Ministry by Inspiration   56

Plain Scriptural Support   57

Christ's Ministers Are True Witnesses, Speaking from
Experience   57

Free Ministry Is the Mark of Christ's Ministers   58

An Objection Answered   59

Chapter 11   **65**

Against Tithes   65

Against All Swearing   65

Against All War among Christians   66

Against the Greetings of the Times   66

For Plainness in Speech   67

Against Mixed Marriages   67

For Plainness in Apparel and Furnishings and No Sports
   and Pastimes after the Manner of This World   68

On Observing Selected Days   68

On Public Behavior, the Care of the Poor, Marriage, and
   Maintaining Good Order in Our Society   68

Appendix: Bible Verses Cited   **71**

Genesis   71

Leviticus   71

Deuteronomy   72

First Samuel   72

First Kings   72

First Chronicles   72

Nehemiah   73

Esther   73

Job   73

Psalms   74

Proverbs   74

Song of Solomon   75

Isaiah   76

Joel   77

Micah   77

Matthew   78

Mark   79

Luke   80

John   80

Acts   83

Romans   84

First Corinthians   86

Second Corinthians   87

Galatians   88

Ephesians   89

Contents

Philippians   89

Colossians   89

First Thessalonians   90

First Timothy   90

Titus   90

Hebrews   91

James   92

First Peter   92

Second Peter   92

First John   93

Third John   94

Revelation   94

Acknowledgments

This is the second edition of my translation of William Penn's *Primitive Christianity Revived* into modern English. The first edition was part of *Twenty-First Century Penn*, a translation of five of Penn's theological works. That book was published by Earlham School of Religion Publications in 2003. They have given permission for this new edition to be published by Inner Light Books as a companion to *Primitive Quakerism Revived*.

Comments and encouragement from Jay Marshall and Stephen Angell of the Earlham School of Religion helped to keep me focused while I worked on the first edition. In addition, a number of books on Penn and his writings were invaluable in that work. In particular, footnotes in Hugh Barbour's *William Penn on Religion and Ethics* frequently pointed me toward information that I would not have easily found on my own. Barbara Mays was invaluable in reviewing that manuscript and offering many helpful comments.

Charles Martin, the Inner Light Books publisher and editor, and his copy editor, Kathy McKay, have been very helpful in the process of revision. He also introduced me to David Johnson, an Australian Quaker, who read a draft and sent me useful comments.

But most importantly, my wife Peggy Spohr has again endured my long hours of contemplation on the ultimate meaning of three-hundred-and-fifty-year-old words—keeping me appropriately clothed, fed, and rested. I could not have done it without her.

Translator's Preface

William Penn's *Primitive Christianity Revived* was published in 1696. Penn had been writing Quaker defenses for thirty years, but this one was different. As a young convert, his writing had been passionate, even intemperate. Among other things, he claimed that Quakers were the only true Christians. In 1668, he had been thrown into the Tower of London and charged with blasphemy for what he had written. Thirty years later, Penn wrote *Primitive Christianity Revived* as a Christian writing to other Christians who were not Quaker. It was a short introduction to Quakerism—a moderate and reasoned argument aimed at persuading others that Friends had restored Christianity to its original form as established by Jesus and the apostles, but he no longer charged others with being "pretended Christians."

This is my second attempt to render William Penn's *Primitive Christianity Revived* in modern English. The first edition was part of *Twenty-First Century Penn*, which I was inspired to write by my repeated and unsuccessful attempts to read Penn's works in their original formats. I began each attempt convinced that the contents were so important that my education in Quaker Studies would be incomplete without them. Each time, I foundered on Penn's seventeenth-century language. He had received a gentleman's education. Even before becoming a Quaker, he had trained in theology at Saumur, a Reformed seminary in France, and had read the law at Lincoln's Inn in London. His sentences were long, intricate, and full of words with unfamiliar meanings. I needed to carefully translate each one before I could read it.

Years of contemplation of William Penn's writings in turn recently inspired me to write *Primitive Quakerism Revived*, a book aimed at contemporary Quakers. In writing that book, I reviewed my work on Penn. After fifteen years, some of my word choices seemed imprecise or even inaccurate. The format I had used—including each referenced scripture passage as a footnote—led to a cluttered appearance, and I found more than enough typos to justify a new edition.

Truth, Revelation, and Apostasy

Before beginning to read the text below, it may be helpful to review a few of Penn's basic religious concepts. Perhaps the most important of these is that Penn believed in Truth with a capital 'T.' Not only did ultimate truth exist, but it was humanly knowable—although never in its entirety.

Penn saw the history of God's interactions with humanity as the story of continuing divine revelation. In each succeeding age, people could come to know more and more of God's Truth. The Bible records a series of dispensations or ways in which God interacts with humanity, but the Scriptures only record the revelations to Jews and Christians. Penn was convinced that God does not abandon any part of humanity—God's will has been revealed to all people in all ages through the work of the Light within each individual soul.

But the story is not so simple. Central to Penn's understanding of God's dealings with humanity was a theory of apostasy. Briefly stated, this theory held that in each age God would gather a people and reveal a measure of truth to them. In each case, they would remain faithful to that revelation for a period of time, but inevitably they would fall away from it. Apostasy would supplant true religion as people substituted their own ideas for those they had received from God. Temptation to apostasy was the continual work of the devil, and only unrelenting spiritual warfare could overcome it.

Friends were persecuted for much of the second half of the seventeenth century, and the pressures of persecution drove them, under the political leadership of William Penn, to seek religious toleration from the government. In promoting this goal, Penn distinguished between 'essential' and 'nonessential' aspects of faith and practice. He argued that the outward differences that distinguished Quakers from other Christians were neither essential nor necessary and, therefore, should not be points of contention. In *Primitive Christianity Revived*, he attempted to describe what was essential for a Christian and how Friends were fulfilling that role.

The Bible

It is important when reading Penn to understand how people viewed the Bible in the seventeenth century. English culture and society was steeped in the Scriptures. Beginning late in the previous century, English-language Bibles had been printed in great numbers and had become readily available to common people. The Bible was the only book many had ever read, and the stories and language of the Bible were familiar to all.

Penn could assume that his readers were quite familiar with the King James Version of the Bible. Even those who had not or could not read the Bible themselves were well acquainted with its contents. As a result, he could quote a passage, or use just a few words, and assume that readers would identify the reference and know its context. Such an assumption can no longer be made. To give modern readers a sense of this way of reading, I have provided relevant scriptural references parenthetically in the text. Penn rarely quoted the Scriptures directly; usually he would use a few words from a verse and count on the reader to fill in the rest. In some cases, he would provide a reference in the margin, but often he did not. I have added citations where it seems clear he is alluding to a particular section. In modernizing the language in Penn's quotations from Scripture, I have made use of a number of contemporary versions of the Bible as well as of the original Greek and Hebrew texts. My intention, however, is not to provide the best possible translation of the text but to come as close as possible to Penn's intentions.

All cited excerpts from the Bible can be found in the appendix. Although I have translated Penn's text (including biblical verses) into modern English, I felt that the flavor of his book is better represented by presenting the biblical verses in the appendix in the language of the King James Version.

The Translation

Penn wrote prolifically, publishing more than one hundred books and pamphlets on topics ranging from law, politics, and international relations to business, education, and science and on to philosophy and theology. For one hundred and fifty years after his death, his works were definitive among Friends, sitting beside *The Journal of George Fox* and Robert Barclay's *Apology*. While *The Journal* has remained in print and Dean Freiday's *Barclay's Apology in Modern English* has revived interest in that work, Penn's theological works have fallen from favor. In large measure, this is due to Penn's background and training. He was an English gentleman, trained in theology and the law, and he wrote like a theologian and lawyer. His sentences are long and involved. In addition, his word choices are often unfamiliar to modern readers—sometimes a word will look familiar, but its meaning has changed in the nearly three hundred years since his death.

In this volume, I have attempted to overcome these barriers by treating his original work as if it was written in a foreign language. What is presented below is simply a "translation" into modern English. To the best of my ability, I have retained Penn's concepts while putting them in words that a twenty-first-century reader can easily understand. As with any translation, I have had to make choices. Although most English words have retained their meanings over the last three hundred years, in some cases the primary meaning of a word is now very different.

For example, consider the word 'prove.' If I say that I am going to prove a proposition, most people today would understand that I am aiming to demonstrate that the idea is true. In the seventeenth century, the same phrase would be understood to mean that I was going to test the truth of the proposition—that it may or may not be true. Thus, for example, the old saying "The exception proves the rule" didn't mean that finding an exception shows a proposed rule to be true. The existence of an exception tests the validity of the rule.

Two terms in Penn's writings could particularly mislead a modern reader. 'Evangelical' has taken on new meanings since the 1800s. In twenty-first-century America, it is used to describe Protestants who read the Bible as the ultimate authority, believe in Jesus Christ as Lord and Savior, and emphasize a personal relationship with Jesus Christ. When Penn used the term, however, he was referring to the gospel. Thus, an evangelical history is a gospel, an evangelist is a gospel writer, and the evangelical prophet (or beloved disciple) is the Apostle John.

Likewise, in the last several centuries the word 'universalism' has come to be understood in religious circles as the belief that everyone will be saved. William Penn, however, lived in a time when most people believed that salvation was possible only for a chosen few. Early Friends rejected such claims. For them, the universal infusion of the Light proclaimed in John 1:9 ("*That* was the true Light, which lighteth every man that cometh into the world" in the King James Version) creates the possibility, but not the promise, of salvation for all. The death of Jesus on the cross made salvation universally possible for everyone—Christian, Jew, Muslim, pagan, or atheist—but didn't guarantee it. That could be achieved only by faithfully following the guidance of the Inward Light. To avoid confusion, I have usually replaced 'universal' with other words.

Standards of punctuation and capitalization have changed considerably over the last three hundred years. As part of the translation, I have made the punctuation conform to modern standards, but I have retained some of Penn's original capitalization. As noted above, Penn distinguished between ordinary truth and ultimate truth. Where he is referring to ultimate Truth, it is spelled with a capital 'T.' Likewise, words that are used as a name of God or that describe attributes of God (e.g., Wisdom, the Word, and the Light) are capitalized. In a few cases, Penn used capitals for emphasis, and some of these have been retained.

Some aspects of Penn's writing may be unattractive, even offensive, to modern readers. Seventeenth-century English society was defined by a rigid class structure that Penn and virtually all his contemporaries saw as natural and even as ordained by God. The roles of men and women; masters, servants, and slaves; and nobility, gentry, and commoners were well known, understood, and accepted. The superiority of Christianity to Judaism (and certainly to any other religion) was taken for granted. In the translation below, I have made an effort to avoid unnecessarily exclusive or offensive language—such as the use of male pronouns for God—but this cannot be done entirely without reducing the value of this work by distorting the view it gives us of Penn, his times, and his message.

Penn wrote *Primitive Christianity Revived* to challenge its original readers, both Quaker and non-Quaker. It presented an evolving understanding of how God relates to humanity and how the Religious Society of Friends should relate to the world surrounding it. More than *The Journal of George Fox* or Robert Barclay's *Apology*, Penn's books set the direction for the development of that faith community for the next one hundred and fifty years and, consequently, for the shape of that religious body today.

An Epistle to the Reader

Reader,

By this short treatise, you will come to understand that the Light of Christ in each person is the manifestation of God's love for our happiness. This is the unique testimony and characteristic of the people called Quakers. It is their most fundamental principle—distinguishing them from all other Christians of this time—and, in their ministry and writing, is the basis for their faith, worship, and practice. They hold that just as fingers grow naturally out of the hand or branches out of the trunk of a tree, so all aspects of true religion grow out of this Divine Principle.

Some are greatly prejudiced against this people; others admire Quakers for their seriousness and principled lives but, out of misunderstanding or ignorance, believe them to be wrong on important points of doctrine. But there are many more, within every other denomination, who earnestly desire to know and delight in God directly, as these people describe it. They long for a state of holiness and acceptance by God but despair of ever attaining it. Because they have not felt the inward power that God has given them or experienced it working within them, enabling them to attain that state, they doubt its reality.

For these reasons, Reader, I have decided to write a short tract about the nature and power of the Inward Light of Christ, explaining what and where it is and the purposes it serves. In so doing, I will describe the religion of the people called Quakers so everyone may know their true character, what true religion is, and how to practice that true religion in this age of hypocrisy and perverted belief. I am writing so the merciful visitations of the God of Light and Love, which efficiently and directly promote piety (which is true religion), will no longer be ignored in our nations. Rather, all may come to believe with their hearts and confess with their mouths (Romans 10:9) that this is the dispensation of Love and Life from God to the whole world. Moreover, you will see that this poor people called Quakers—so despised, so often maligned and treated as the scum of the earth—are the people of God and the children of the Most High.

Bear with me, Reader. I know what I am saying—I am not arrogant, but truly God-fearing. Though I write with confidence toward you, it is with humility toward God. But don't take my word alone—don't act on trust but on knowledge. Judge what I write carefully. That is all I ask and all I need to convince you and to vindicate myself. Take this tract as a spiritual inquiry into and for your soul. It requires no faith in outward authority but is obvious to anyone who honestly examines it.

Reader, when you become familiar with this Divine Principle and its plain and joyful teachings, like us, you will be amazed you did not long ago see the truth of something so close to you. In the past, you thought us strange for believing; soon you will wonder why others are so blind to it. The time, I believe, is at hand when all will accept this unquestionable evidence and declare the absolute authority of this principle.

Let me finish this preface with a brief description of my plan. First, I will state the Divine Principle and demonstrate to you (as God has enabled me) its nature and power in religion. In doing so, the common doctrines and principles of Christianity will be presented and explained for your benefit in a straightforward manner. In this, I have tried to use only plain and simple terms—not figurative, allegorical, or ambiguous phrases—so there will be no room for misunderstanding, equivocation, or double meanings. The truth of this matter will be evident and easily understood by everyone. Second, each point will be supported by Scripture, reason, and the effects it has had on the lives of so many people. Their consistent faithfulness, at all times and despite sufferings on account of this principle, may challenge the beliefs of serious readers. Third, I have written briefly so this book will be inexpensive and quickly read. Putting as much as possible into a few words seemed best—as people grow richer, they seem to have less time and money for God or religion. Perhaps those who would not buy a large book will find it in their hearts to purchase and give away such little and cheap ones for their neighbors' benefit.

Be serious, Reader, be impartial, and then be as inquisitive as you are able—as much for your own soul as for the credibility of this most misunderstood and abused people. And may God the Father of Lights and Spirits (James 1:17, Hebrews 12:9) bless you as you read this short treatise so that you may receive real benefit from it, to God's glory and to your spiritual comfort. This is my only desire or reason for writing it. In the bonds of Christian charity, I am very much and very ardently,

Thy real Friend,

William Penn

Chapter 1

Friends' Fundamental Principle

For the people called Quakers, the foundation of all religious belief is this: God, through Christ, has placed a guide in each person to show them their duty and has provided each with the ability to follow that guide. In every nation, race, and religion, there are those who follow this guide—these are the people of God—and those who live in disobedience to it and are not God's people regardless of what they say. This is the Friends' ancient, first, and unchanging principle. This is the testimony they have made and will continue to make to the whole world.

The Nature of This Principle

Friends understand this guide as divine. Although it is found within all people, it does not belong to them. It is from God and of God. For those who will let it, it will lead them back to God.

The Names Given This Principle

There are many names for this Divine Principle. By some, it is called the Light of Christ or the Light Within (John 1:9), which is the oldest, most common, and most familiar phrase. Others call it the Revelation (Romans 1:19, Titus 3:4) or Appearance of Christ (Acts 17:28), the Witness of God (Romans 8:16, 1 John 5:10, 12), the Seed of God (1 Peter 1:23, 1 John 3:9) or the Seed of the Kingdom (Matthew 13:19, 23). Still others identify it as Wisdom (Proverbs 1:20-23, 8:1-4), the Word in the Heart (Deuteronomy

30:12-14, Romans 10:6-8, Psalms 119:10), the Grace Available to All (Titus 2:11-12), the Spirit Sent for Each Person's Benefit (1 Corinthians 12:7), the Truth Within (Psalms 51:6, Isaiah 26:2, John 14:6), or the Leaven that Transforms the Lump of Humanity (Matthew 13:33). Many of these are figurative expressions, but all have been used by the inspiration of the Holy Spirit. They will be used in this treatise since they are frequently found in Friends' writings and ministry. But, Reader, do not be misled or confused by the diversity of terms—please remember that when you see any of these terms, it always refers to the one, unchanging Divine Principle I have mentioned above. As I have said, it is in us, not of us, but of God; and although inspired writers have called it by many names in relating its various manifestations and actions, it is One.

Faith and Practice, Ministry and Worship

It is to this Principle of Light, Life, and Grace that Friends refer all. They identify it as the single great active force in religion, without which there is no conviction, no conversion, no rebirth (John 3:5), and, consequently, no entry into the kingdom of God. By conviction, I mean a true recognition of one's own sinfulness and sorrow for it. This is necessary to spur people to conversion—giving up a sinful life and overcoming evil. Without conviction and conversion, people can expect no forgiveness of sin and no justification from it—that is, acceptance by God and peace within the soul—no sanctification or becoming virtuous, holy, or good. Without justification and sanctification, there is no salvation.

Indeed, the reason there is so little true religion among those who call themselves Christians—so much superstition instead of devotion, so little enjoyment in practicing their faith, and so little real change in their hearts—is that people overlook and neglect this principle in their religious lives. They claim to be faithful without it and to be Christians without it, but without it, they are neither.

In this degenerate state, it is natural for people to prefer ritual over obedience, to believe rote words are prayer, and to hope outward ceremonies will reconcile them with God. In that corrupt state, it is only natural people will excuse themselves from the requirements of this principle: taking up their cross, giving up their bodily comforts, and doing whatever God requires of them. This is true religion—to be holy, humble, patient, meek, merciful, just, kind, and charitable. Everyone who is truly religious acts these ways, but they cannot achieve this by their own efforts, only by embracing what the Light reveals and teaches them. This Divine Principle is the root of all true religion and the good seed from which all good fruit grows.

To sum up what Friends have said about the nature and qualities of the Light, this principle is divine, universal and effective in granting humanity the following:

first, knowledge of God and of themselves, and consequently an understanding of themselves, their duty to God, and of their disobedience to God;

second, a true sense of and sorrow for sin in those who seriously consider what the Light shows them;

third, the ability to give up sin and be sanctified from it;

fourth, through God's mercy in Christ, forgiveness of past sins and justification for all who sincerely offer repentance and obedience; and

fifth, the ability for the faithful to persevere, leading them to perfection and the assurance of everlasting blessedness.

Friends offer three things in evidence of the truth of this claim: first, the ample witness of the Scriptures, especially the New Testament; second, the self-evident reasonableness of it; and lastly, the spiritual experience of all people and, in particular, their own. The truth of this experience has been demonstrated in the fruits of their ministry and the results God has granted in answer to that ministry.

These are acknowledged by all impartial observers. In the rest of this work, I will briefly outline the history of Friends to illustrate these points.

Chapter 2

Evidence in Scripture

I will begin with the evidence in the blessed Scriptures of Truth for this Divine Principle. The foremost and most common name used in them to express and name this principle is 'Light'—a most apt and proper word given the current dark state of the world.

> In the beginning was the Word, and the Word was with God, and the Word was God. . . . Through him, all things were made, and without him nothing was made that has been made. In him was Life, and that Life was the Light of all . . . the true Light, which lights everyone that comes into the world. (John 1:1, 3-4, 9)

The Divinity of the Light

I have begun with the Apostle John, the most beloved disciple of Jesus and the last of the apostles to die. Because of his preeminent knowledge and wisdom of heavenly things, he is properly called John the Divine.

John's gospel starts with the beginning of creation by God. He tells us, "In the beginning was the Word," and although that should make it apparent who that Word would be, he goes on to explain the Word was with God and was God. This should remove any doubt about the divinity of the Word or any underestimation of its importance. The Word is divine, and the evangelist chose that term because it so clearly expresses the wisdom and power of God.

All Things Created by the Word

All things were made by him. If that is so, then there is no lack of power. And if we were made by the Word, we must be remade by that same Word or we will never come into joyful union with God. The power of the Word shows its dignity and demonstrates that nothing is impossible for the One who made all things and without which nothing was made. Just as our Maker is our spouse (Isaiah 54:5), so our Creator is our redeemer (Isaiah 44:24).

What the Light Has to Do with Salvation

In him was Life, and that Life was the Light of all. This is precisely our point. John starts with the nature of the existence of the Word and continues on to the works of the Word. Then he tells us how the Word is connected to humanity beyond the rest of creation—the Word was Life, and the Life was the Light of all. This relationship must be very close and intimate if the Life of the Word (which was with God and was God) is the Light of all humanity. This is said of no other creature—as if humanity were next to the Word and above the rest of creation.

Accordingly, humanity does not lack Light—a Divine Light (if the Life of the Divine Word is not divine or supernatural, then nothing can be). And, this text proves not only the divinity of the Light but also its universality—applying to all humanity. This is most directly stated in the ninth verse, "the true Light, which lights everyone that comes into the world." This implies that anything that fails to enlighten all of humanity is not that true Light. Therefore, John was not that Light but only testified to the one who was (John 1:8)—the one who enlightens everyone, the Word that became flesh (John 1:14). In this way, the divine nature and the universality of the Inward Light of Christ are proved together.

Chapter 3

How This Scripture Is Distorted

No passage or proposition to be found in the Scriptures is of greater interest to humanity or more clearly set down by the Holy Spirit than the one I have reported. But, there is also none that has been more ingeniously distorted from its true and plain meaning—especially since Quakers began to stress it in defense of their testimony of the Light Within. Some claim John was writing about a natural light or some part of our own human nature. But it was the true Life of the Word by which the world was made, and these verses are embedded in a section concerned with God's eternal power and the Word's place within the Godhead. So that I can be clearly understood, I will state each objection as clearly as I can and then give an answer to it.

The Claim That It Is a Natural Light

If by 'natural' they mean a created thing, as a person or anything that makes up a person, then I reject their contention. The text expressly refutes it, saying the Light with which all humanity is lighted is the Life of the Word, which was with God and was God.

On the other hand, they may mean simply that the Light comes along with us into the world or that we have it as surely as we are born. That is to say, it is the light of our nature—of our minds and understandings—not the result of any revelation from outside ourselves by other people or by angels. Then we mean the same thing, since it is *natural* for each person to have a *supernatural* Light and for each creature to be lighted by an *uncreated* Light—this is the Life of the *Creating Word*.

If people would simply acknowledge their own nature, it would do much to dispel any confusion about this. A person can no more be a Light to his or her own mind than to his or her own body. People can see an object with the help of light but are not themselves the light that makes an object visible. Just as the sun in the sky is the light of the body, allowing us to see in our everyday lives, the Life of the Word is the glorious Light and sun of the soul. It illuminates our intellects, enlightening our minds and granting us true judgment and discernment about those things that most immediately concern our better, inward, and eternal selves.

The Claim That Not All Are Enlightened

Others assert that the text says that all "who are enlightened" are enlightened by the Word. This not only distorts the text by narrowing its meaning but also portrays God as unfair and unjust, leaving the greatest part of the world in darkness, without any means or opportunity to find salvation. But the Scriptures assure us that all have the Light (John 1:4, 9); that Christ is the Light of the World (John 8:12); that Christ died for all (2 Corinthians 5:15)—even for the ungodly (Romans 5:6); that God does not desire the death of any but rather that all should repent, come to know the Truth, and be saved (1 Timothy 2:4); and that the Grace of God has appeared to all (Titus 2:11-12), etc.

The Claim That It Is the Doctrine and the Example of Christ's Life That Enlightens

There is still a third group that claims that humanity is enlightened and saved not by the Light of Christ but by the doctrine Christ preached, the life he led in the world, and the example he set for us. Yet, not even one-thousandth of humanity has heard these doctrines or knows about his life. Moreover, this claim directly contradicts John's clear message at the beginning of his gospel. This consists entirely of the story of Christ before he became flesh or, at least, the story of what Christ is to the soul by his direct illumination and influence.

It is true that Christ was a Light to the World—'shining forth' in his heavenly doctrine, his many miracles, and his self-denying life and death—but this does not diminish the fact that he was and is that Spiritual Light that shines in one degree or another in the hearts of all of humankind's sons and daughters. Remember that Christ told his disciples, "You are the lights of the world" (Matthew 5:14). In the same (although more powerful) way, his life and teachings are a Light to the world. But Christ the Word enlightened those disciples, enlightens us, and enlightens everyone who comes into the world (John 1:9). It is not his personal and outward life at a time long since passed that continually illuminates those who come into the world. In the flesh, he is remote from us; but in Truth, he is present and immediate. Otherwise, the scriptural text would be, "That was the true Light that used to enlighten all" rather than "the true Light that enlightens all." Indeed, the evangelist uses this as evidence that Christ, not John the Baptist, for whom many had great reverence, is the Messiah. In verse 8, he writes of John the Baptist, "He himself was not the Light, but he came as a witness to the Light." Going on, the next verse provides the proof (and our testimony), "That was the true Light, which lights everyone who comes into the world": not John the Baptist nor any other person but the Word that was with God and was God (John 1:1).

John does not describe Christ as a man who fasted for forty days, preached so many sermons, worked so many miracles, lived a holy life, and, after all that, patiently suffered death (as Christ did) in order to prove he was the Light of the World. No. John begins by writing that Christ was the true Light, the Word made flesh (John 1:14), the Messiah, and that neither John the Baptist nor any other person enlightens everyone who comes into the world. Right from the start, Christ alone is distinguished and revealed by giving Light. What is more, his followers are distinguished from all other people by receiving and obeying that Light.

Many other relevant passages in both testaments refer implicitly and explicitly to the Light Within. For brevity, I will not recite them all, but some of them are Job 18:5-6, Job 21:17, Job 25:3, Job 38:15, Psalms 18:28, Psalms 27:1, Psalms 34:5, Psalms 36:9, Psalms 118:27, Psalms 119:105, Proverbs 13:9, Proverbs 20:20 and 27, Proverbs 24:20, Isaiah 2:5, Isaiah 8:20, Isaiah 42:6, Isaiah 49:6, 1 Peter 2:9, and 1 John 2:8.

Chapter 4

The Power of the Inward Light to Grant Discernment

C onsider the power and effectiveness of the Light to achieve the purpose for which God has given it—to lead and guide human souls to blessedness. The first thing it does, in accomplishing this, is to give a person true insight into, or discernment of, themselves—the ability to know who they truly are and what they do—so they may see and know their own spiritual condition. By this, they know what judgment to make of themselves with respect to religion and a future state. As the unerring Word says and John reports, everyone who does evil hates the Light and avoids the Light so their wicked deeds will not be exposed. But those who live by the Truth come to the Light so all might see that everything they do has been done in God (John 3:20-21). This is a most compelling expression of the power and authority of the Light!

First, the Light is identified as that by which we must examine ourselves. Second, it allows us to accurately discern the differences between good and evil—what is of God and what is not of God. Third, it is a judge who acquits or condemns—rejecting those who reject it and comforting the souls of those who obey it. Only something that is itself divine can reveal to us what comes of God and what does not or permit us to see what within ourselves has been fashioned by the hand of God and what has not. This passage is concerned not only with revealing a person's inner state but, what is more, with an understanding of God and the works of God. It tells us that each person who is obedient can also come to know, to some degree, which acts are performed by the power of God and according to the will of God and which are the products of her or his own will.

If the Light did not reveal God, it could not tell us what God's will is for us nor give us a well-grounded sense and discernment of the origin, nature, and tendencies of our own minds and of our innermost being. Certainly, this is both explicitly expressed and abundantly implied by our Savior in this passage. And if the Light reveals God, we can be sure that it makes Christ, who flows from and comes from God, known to us. Who then would oppose or rebuff this blessed Light?

The Light Reveals God

That this Light reveals God is evident in Romans 1:19, "For what can be known about God is plain to them, because God has shown it to them." This is a universal proposition, and we have the apostle's word for it—the word of a man who was one in a thousand and inspired by the Holy Spirit to tell us Truth. Let us grant it its due importance. If what can be known about God "is plain to them," then the people called Quakers certainly cannot be going astray when they extol the Light Within. Without that Light, nothing can be made known to our minds.

Remember that the same apostle wrote to the Ephesians, "Everything that is condemned is revealed by the Light—whatever reveals is Light" (Ephesians 5:13). Since the Light Within reveals in us and to us everything that may be known of God, it is rightly called a revelation or appearance of God. Similarly, the Prophet Micah tells us, "God has shown you, O mortal, what is good; and what does the Lord require of you but to do justice, and to love mercy, and to walk humbly with your God?" (Micah 6:8). I repeat: "God has shown you, O mortal!" This is very emphatic. And how has God shown us? By God's Light in our consciences, "against which the wicked rebel"—those who, "for whatever cause, do not know its ways, and do not stay in its paths" (Job 24:13). But, to those who do obey, "its ways are ways of pleasantness, and all its paths are peace" (Proverbs 3:17).

The Light Gives Life to the Soul

The Light gives the Light of Life—in other words, it grants eternal life to those who receive it and obey it. For this, we have the word of the blessed Savior of the World, "I am the Light of the World. Whoever follows me will never walk in darkness but will have the Light of Life" (John 8:12). Christ is the Light of the World because he enlightens everyone who comes into the world (John 1:9), and those who obey that Light obey him and therefore have the Light of Life. That is to say, the Light becomes eternal life to the soul. Just as it is the Life of the Word, which is the Light in humanity, so God's heavenly Light becomes Life in humanity through our obedience to it.

The Light Is the Apostolic Message

Furthermore, this Light was the foundation of the apostolic message. As the beloved disciple assures us,

> This is the message we have heard from him and proclaim to you: God is Light and in him there is no darkness at all. If we say that we have fellowship with him while we are walking in darkness, we lie and are not doing the truth; but if we walk in the Light as he himself is in the Light, we have fellowship with one another, and the blood of Jesus his Son cleanses us from all sin. (1 John 1:5-7)

This passage so amply demonstrates the surpassing value and power of the Light as it applies to humanity that there is little need to say any more. It says, first, that the Light reveals God and that God is Light. Second, it distinguishes darkness from Light and the fact that the two have nothing in common (2 Corinthians 6:14). Third, it tells us we should walk in the Light; fourth, that walking in the Light is the way to obtain forgiveness for sin and sanctification from sin; and fifth, that the Light is the instrument of peace and fellowship with God and with God's people—the true church, which is saved from all the pollutions of the world.

An Objection About Two Lights Answered

Perhaps some will object, as has happened more than once before, that this is another light, not the Light with which all are enlightened. But the same apostle, in his evangelical history, tells us that in the Word was Life; the Life was the Light of all people—the Light being the Life of the Word; and that Light was the true Light, which enlightens all who come into the world. Could there be a plainer text to support the sufficiency and universality of the Light Within? Is there a plainer statement of any article of faith in the whole of the Book of God? If the beloved disciple had intended to indicate there were two Lights, in either his gospel or epistles, we can be sure he would have made the distinction—but we find none and, from the properties attributed to the Light in each of his writings, we have good reason to conclude he intended only one.

Natural and Spiritual Light: There Are neither Two Darknesses nor Two Lights

Still, there may be those who object that John writes of a Spiritual Light but ours is only a natural one. I ask them just two things: First, prove that a natural light, as they put it, can reveal God. Whatever is part of our own being and nature, especially in our fallen state, is so far from God that it cannot rightly reveal or reject those things that offend God. But the Light we have written about, which we call divine and others mistakenly call natural, can do both.

Second, if this Light is natural, it still seems to show us our duty and to rebuke us for our disobedience to God. That being the case, those who object need to identify the means by which we can correctly discern and distinguish between the revelations and reproofs of a natural light within and those of the Divine Light Within—since they propose both are capable of discovering God and condemning evil. Let them show us one passage in Scripture that distinguishes between a natural and a Spiritual Light Within. They might as well talk about a natural and a spiritual darkness within. There is, of course, a natural and proper darkness—the night of the outward world—and a spiritual darkness—the clouded and benighted human conceptions that result from disobeying the Light and Spirit of God. But, there is no third form of darkness. People improperly used to say the blind were dark, and some have also used that term to describe those who are mentally impaired, but is there another kind of darkness in understanding the things of God?

Neither Christ nor his disciples ever distinguished between one kind of darkness and another nor, in any sense, between two kinds of Light. Yet, all spoke of Light and darkness. The Scriptures often address darkness (consider, for example, Luke 1:79; Matthew 4:16; John 1:5, 3:19, 8:12, 31, 46; 1 Thessalonians 5:4; 1 John 1:6; Acts 26:18; Romans 13:12; 2 Corinthians 6:14; Ephesians 5:8; Colossians 1:13), but on the closest examination of these verses, there is no distinction made between different kinds. There is only one spiritual darkness. Nor is there a single verse that distinguishes different forms of the Light Within or indicates that there are really two Lights from God with respect to religion (consider, for example, Matthew 4:16; Luke 2:32, 15:8; John 1:4-9, 3:19-21, 8:12; Acts 26:18; Romans 13:12; 2 Corinthians 4:6, 6:14; Ephesians 5:8,13; Colossians 1:12; 1 Thessalonians 5:5; 1 Timothy 6:16; 1 Peter 2:9; 1 John 1:5, 7; 1 John 2:8; Revelation 21:23-24, 22:5).

And we believe the most skilled of our opponents will not be able to sever Light from Light or to find two Lights Within in the passages I have listed or in any other passage that directs us in our duties to God or to our neighbors. If so, then we ask them to give up their unworthy thoughts and words about the Light of Christ within all and acknowledge that the Light reveals evil and condemns it. As Christ himself teaches, "All who do evil hate the Light and do not come to the Light so that their deeds may not be exposed" (John 3:20). And, as the Apostle Paul wrote, "All things that are condemned are exposed by the Light" (Ephesians 5:13). There are not two distinct Lights Within—there is only one exposing, condemning, and teaching Light Within. And the Apostle John, in his first epistle, makes this plain, beyond all question, to any reasonable person. First, he declares God is Light, saying there is no darkness within God (1 John 1:5). Second, there is no middle way between Light and darkness—we must walk either in Light or in darkness; there is no other alternative. Everyone must agree that whatever reveals and condemns darkness cannot be darkness itself.

The Objection Is Fully Answered by the Apostle John

It is as if John had anticipated their next objection, i.e., that while the Light Within reveals evil, it is not necessarily the Divine Light, which leads us to higher things and which comes by the gospel. The apostle wrote, "The darkness is passing away and the true Light is already shining. Anyone who says, 'I am in the Light' while hating a brother or sister is still in the darkness" (1 John 2:8-9). The Light is here shown in opposition to darkness, and the darkness is in opposition to Light. This is the same Light John mentioned in the previous chapter. The darkness is the same; the Light is also the same. Plainly, there is one Light that rebukes a person for hating a brother or sister and that brings us into fellowship with God and to the cleansing blood—this is the Light of a divine and effective nature. In short, the Light that is opposite to and condemns spiritual darkness in a man or a woman is a spiritual Light. This is what the Quakers believe, testify, and maintain.

It is also worth noticing that the apostle uses the same expression here, "The true Light is shining," as he does in the first chapter of his gospel, "That was the true Light" (John 1:9). This indicates that the same Divine Word or True Light now shines. The Light that calls to account those who hate a brother or sister is the same True Light that enlightens all. Is it not remarkable that Christ and his disciples—most especially his beloved one—would so often equate the Light that reveals to us our least indiscretion and condemns our grossest evil with the Divine Life itself? That Light, revealed more and more, calls us to follow it to the Light of Life, to the cleansing blood, and to fellowship with God and with one another. Beyond that, the apostle declares that to be a child of God we must answer this Light in an obvious and ordinary way: by not hating our brothers or sisters. How could anyone shut their eyes so tightly that they cannot see the power such a Light must have? How could anyone describe this Light as natural or insufficient for salvation? To do so is unreasonable and unscriptural.

Is the Light dismissed as unimportant because it is so familiar, so ordinary, and so abundantly available to us? Do we underestimate its immeasurable mercy simply because of that abundance? What could be more common than light, air, and water? Should we disdain them or prize them? No doubt we prize them, knowing we cannot live without them. The more widely mercy is offered, the greater it is, and consequently the greater our obligation to be grateful and to live humbly in return. To those who do so, the divine secrets of the Light are revealed.

Chapter 5

The Light Is the Same as the Spirit of God

S ome may object that everything we have attributed to the Light is properly the work of the Spirit and Grace of God. These, they say, are the unique blessings of the New and Second Covenant and are the fruits of the coming of Christ. Unless, they say, the Light has the same nature as the Spirit and Grace of God, they cannot bring themselves to believe what we have said.

At first glance, this objection seems to carry some weight, but on careful reflection, it will be seen to have more appearance than substance. Even so, because it provides the opportunity to remove some stumbling blocks that may be thrown in the way of the unsophisticated, I will answer it thoroughly. If it can be shown that the properties of the Light Within are the same as those of the Spirit and Grace of God, then it will be obvious we are only using different names to describe the various manifestations or operations of the one and the same ultimate Divine Principle. Following the objectors' logic, this will prove our claim that the Light is divine and is sufficient to lead people to salvation.

Let us examine the claim that the Light Within is of the same nature as the Spirit and Grace of God and produces the same result, that is, bringing people to God. First, the Light originates in the One Word and the One Life of that Word, which was with God and was God (John 1:1, 4). Second, it is universal— enlightening all (John 1:9). Third, it gives knowledge of and communion with God (Romans 1:19; John 3:21; 1 John 1:5-6). Fourth, it reveals and condemns evil (John 3:20; Ephesians 5:13). Fifth, it is named as the rule and guide for Christian behavior (Psalms 43:3; John 8:12; Ephesians 5:13, 15). Sixth, it is the path for God's people to follow; the nations of those who are saved will walk in the Light of the Lamb (Psalms 119:105; Proverbs 4:18; Isaiah 2:5; 1 John 1:7; Revelation 21:23-24). Lastly, it is the armor of the children of God against Satan. "The LORD is my Light; whom shall I fear?" (Psalms 27:1; Romans 13:12).

The Properties of the Light and the Spirit Compared

If all this is compared with the properties of the Spirit, the agreement will be immediately obvious. First, the Spirit originates in God because it is the Spirit of God.* Second, it is universal. It struggled to help us in the old world of the Law (Genesis 6:3) and again in the new world of grace in which everyone has received a measure of it (1 Corinthians 12:7). Third, it reveals God (Job 32:8; 1 Corinthians 2:10-11). Fourth, it condemns sin (John 16:8). Fifth, it is a rule and guide for the children of God to follow (Romans 8:14). Sixth, it is also the path they are to walk in (Romans 8:1; Galatians 5:16)—"Walk in the Spirit." And this is not all. It is, lastly, the spiritual weapon of the true Christian—"Take the sword of the Spirit, which is the Word of God" (Ephesians 6:17). After this, I hope no one will deny that this Light and this Spirit must be of one and the same nature, that they produce one and the same effect, and that they clearly point to one and the same holy result.

---

* Penn included a reference to Romans 6:11 in the text, but this verse has no apparent connection to the point his is making.

The Light and the Spirit Flow from the Same Source

What is said of the Light and the Spirit may equally be said of the Light and Grace of God. First, Grace, like the Light, flows from Christ, the Word that became flesh. Just as in him was Life and that Life was the Light of humanity, so was he also full of Grace and Truth, and from that fullness we have all received one blessing after another (John 1:4, 9, 14, 16). Second, it is universal—as can be seen both in this text and in the epistle to Titus, where Paul taught that the Grace of God that brings salvation has appeared to all (Titus 2:11-12). Third, it reveals evil. If it teaches us to turn away from ungodliness and worldly desires, it must make those things visible to us. Fourth, it reveals godliness and consequently must show us God. Fifth, it is a teacher and guide, providing us with a rule of life—as Paul's letter to Titus has declared. Sixth, to those who accept it, it is all they require or desire (2 Corinthians 12:9): "My Grace is sufficient for you." This is strong testimony from heaven of the power of this teaching and saving grace in the face of the greatest temptations.

An Objection Answered

The objection is raised that there is little mention of the Spirit and none of Grace before Christ's coming. From this, it is claimed that the Spirit as spoken of in the New Testament and Grace even more so must be something separate from and better than the Light Within.

This is easily answered. The Spirit and Grace are by no means different from the Light Within but are merely other names given to different manifestations or actions of the same Eternal Principle. It is called Light because of its property of revealing and the resultant discerning. In the beginning of the old world, God said, "Let there be Light," and there was Light (Genesis 1:3). In the same way, Light is present at the beginning of God's new creation in humanity. It is called Spirit because it gives life, senses, motion, and vigor. And, every reader can see in a concordance that it is often mentioned in the Old Testament, just as it is in the New. For example, God's Spirit struggled with the old world (Genesis 6:3) and with Israel in the wilderness (Nehemiah 9:30). Likewise, David asked in the agony of his soul, "Where can I go from your Spirit?" (Psalms 139:7). And, the prophets often felt it.

It is called Grace not because it is a different thing but because it was a more complete pouring out of the virtue and power of God's favor and mercy. Something that we are not worthy of should be called grace or favor or God's good will when dispensed to an undeserving people. The wind does not always blow fresh, nor the rain fall freely, nor the sun shine brightly. Do we say it is not the same kind of wind, rain, or sunshine when it blows softly, rains gently, or shines only a little rather than blowing powerfully, raining hard, or shining brightly? Certainly each is the same in kind and nature—and so is this Blessed Principle, in all its manifestations and in all its actions for the benefit of souls in every age since the world began.

The Differences in Appearance or Action

We freely, humbly, and thankfully acknowledge that the gospel dispensation is the best, clearest, and fullest of all—both as expressed in Christ's life and in his sacrifice as the one holy offering to God for sin and in the fuller breaking forth of his Light, the bountiful pouring out of his Spirit and the abundant appearance of his Grace in and to humanity after his ascension into heaven. Though it was not a different Light or Spirit than God had given to humanity in earlier times, it was given in greater measure than ever before. That is the advantage of the gospel over the earlier dispensations—what had previously shone only dimly now shines with great glory. Before it appeared darkly, but now it is unveiled for all to see (2 Corinthians 3:18). Types, figures, and shadows hid its appearances and made them look low and faint, but in the gospel time, the veil is torn and the hidden glory is hidden no more (Hebrews 10:20). Under the law, it was available to us like dew or a light rain, but under the gospel, it has been poured out on everyone as the Prophet Joel told us God had promised: "Afterward, I will pour out my Spirit on all people" (Joel 2:28).[*] Thus we say, when it rains, look how it pours. This is how God has expanded Light, Spirit, and Grace in these days. We shall not receive it sparingly in dribs and drabs but fully and freely, even to overflowing. On Pentecost, Peter refers to the promise in Joel, declaring that day to be the beginning of its fulfillment. This is Grace, Favor, and Goodness indeed. This greater illumination and greater pouring forth of the Spirit is rightly called Grace. Just as the appearance of the Son exceeded that of the servant,[†] the appearance of the Light and Spirit of God, since the coming of Christ, exceeds that of all previous dispensations. It is sufficient to lead all who follow it to salvation. This is our understanding of the Light, Spirit, and Grace of God. By what has been said in the Scriptures, it is obvious these are all one and the same Divine Principle. Anyone who with love accepts the Light will not lack the Spirit or Grace of God. All are one: Light to guide us, Spirit to give us Life, and Grace to teach, help, and comfort us. To those who

---

[*] This text is also quoted in Acts 2:17 by Peter in his sermon to the crowds on Pentecost.

[†] This may be a reference to the parable of the Wicked Tenants in Luke 20.

diligently follow and obey it, it is sufficient for every circumstance of our lives.

Chapter 6

Although All Are Enlightened, Not All Are Good

S ome may still say that if it is as we have described, why is it that not all who are enlightened are as good as they should be or as good as we have said this would make them?

The answer is that not all people receive and obey the Inward Light. All have the ability to reason, but not all are reasonable. Is it the fault of grain stored in the granary that it does not grow or of money hidden in a napkin that it does not earn interest?[*] It is obvious when a gift has been given and just as obvious when it could have been used profitably—both because others have used a similar gift to their advantage and because a just lender expects a loan to be repaid with interest (Luke 19:23). So, let those who object tell us whose fault it was that some have wasted their gift. We are prepared to tell them why the unprofitable servant was not as good as he should have been. The blind must not blame the sun for their blindness, nor should sinners accuse Grace of being inadequate. It is sin that darkens the spiritual eyes, hardens the heart, and obstructs all good things. Christ has told us that if we do God's will, we will know God's doctrines (John 7:17). Those who do not live up to what they already have been given cannot blame God for not giving them more. The unfruitfulness is in

---

[*] The reference is to the third servant in the parable of the Three Servants, in particular to Luke 19:20.

them, not in the gift (Mark 4:19). It would be good if they would take this to heart, but, unfortunately, people are too inclined to follow their sensual appetites rather than their reasonable minds. This turns them into dumb brutes rather than rational creatures. The reasonable part in us is our spiritual part—the part guided by the divine *Logos*, or Word. Tertullian* interprets reason, in this most exalted sense, as that which makes people truly reasonable and allows them to offer themselves up to God in spiritual worship (Romans 12:1). Then they are as God first made them—in God's own image—when God gave them a paradise for their home (Genesis 1:26).

Gospel Truths Were Known Before Christ

Others object that if mankind always had access to this Divine Principle, why is it that those who were obedient to it did not know the gospel truths before the coming of Christ?

The answer is simply that a beginning is not the same as an end. A child is not a fully grown adult, but the child at the beginning of a life is the same person as the adult at the end of it. The underlying reality remains the same although its appearance changes. Just as the world has and will have many stages or periods in its history, so does humanity in its progress to perfection. Those who are faithful to God's dispensation in their own time will hear the happy welcome of "Well done, good and faithful servant" (Matthew 25:23).

Even so, many of God's people in those times anticipated the glory of later times—the growth and development of religion and the happiness to come in the church of God. This can be seen in

---

* Tertullian (c. 155–after 220) was an early Christian theologian and moralist.

the prophecies of Jacob and Moses concerning the restoration of Israel by Christ (Genesis 49:10; Deuteronomy 18:15, 18). David, in many of his excellent Psalms, expresses palpable and extraordinary joys as well as prophecies, especially in Psalms 2, 15, 18, 22, 23, 25, 27, 32, 36, 37, 42, 43, 45, 51, and 84. The prophets are similarly full of such anticipation, and this is why they are called prophets; see particularly Isaiah in chapters 2, 9, 11, 25, 28, 32, 35, 42, 49-54, 59-61, 63, and 65-66; Jeremiah in chapters 23, 30-31, and 33; Ezekiel in chapters 20, 34, and 36-37; Daniel in chapters 8-12; Hosea in chapters 1 and 3; Joel in chapters 2-3; Amos in chapter 9; Micah in chapters 4-5; Zachariah in chapters 6, 8, 9, 11, and 13-14; and Malachi in chapters 3-4. They did not write about different things but always about the same Divine Principle—although it had different appearances at different times. Nor did they prophesy in general terms—what they wrote was specific and extraordinary.

The same Spirit that came on Moses came on John the Baptist. The Spirit that came over Gideon and Sampson was the same as the one that fell on Peter and Paul. This doesn't make it the same dispensation of that Spirit—God visits and appears to people in ways appropriate to their spiritual states and conditions and in ways in which they are prepared to receive the Divine Presence, whether it is more outwardly or inwardly, through their senses, or through their spirits. There is no human capacity too great or too small to be touched by this Divine Principle—it made and knows all, so it reaches out to each person in the manner most appropriate. It touches the lowly, and the highest cannot live without it. This is what made David call out in distress to God, "Where can I hide from your Spirit? Where can I flee from your presence?" He implies that God is everywhere—not that God is the same at all times and in all places. "If I go to heaven, you are there; to hell, or beyond the seas, even there your hand will guide me and your right hand will hold me" (Psalms 139:7-10) . In other words, "Wherever I am and wherever I go, this Divine Word, this Light, this Spirit of God, will find me, lead me, help me, and comfort me. It is with me always in one form or another" (Proverbs 6:22; Isaiah 43:2). David knew this and therefore held that knowledge very precious: "In your Light we see Light" (Psalms 36:9). In other words, we will be enlightened by Divine Light. Or, "You light my candle; the Lord, my God, lights up my darkness" (Psalms 18:28), and "The Lord is my Light; whom shall I fear?" (Psalms 27:1). The Light was David's armor against all danger. It took away his fear, and he was undaunted because he was safe in it. Of the same blessed Word, he says elsewhere, "It is a lamp to my feet and a light for my path" (Psalms 119:105). In short, the Light led him in the way of blessedness.

The Gentiles Had the Same Light But without the Same Advantages

The objectors say that just because the Jews had this Light does not mean the Gentiles had it too, whereas our doctrine declares all have it.

We answer yes, our doctrine is exactly that, and it is the glory of our doctrine that it proclaims that God's love is offered to all. Besides the general texts cited above, the Apostle Paul is very specific in the second chapter of his Epistle to the Romans. There he states, "Gentiles, who do not have the law, do naturally things required by the law; they are a law for themselves." That is, they did not have an outward law, as the Jews did, but "the requirements of the law are written on their hearts," which is to say they had the law within themselves to guide them. And the Jews did too, but they had greater outward help to assist them in obeying—help not given to any other nation. Therefore, the obedience of the

Gentiles, or uncircumcised, is said to be by nature only because they did not have the extra, external, and extraordinary ministries and supports available to the Jews. This does not diminish in any way the obedient Gentiles in the apostle's judgment but instead exalts them. Although they did not have those advantages, even so "the requirements of the law written on their hearts" were apparent in the good lives they lived in the world. He adds that every day their consciences witnessed to them and their own thoughts will accuse them or excuse them for their actions on the Day of Judgment (Romans 2:14-16).

This presents us with four things related to our point that are worthy of serious reflection. First, the Gentiles had the law written in their hearts. Second, their consciences were an acceptable witness to their faithfulness in doing their duty. Third, the judgment made on that evidence will be confirmed on the Day of Judgment and is therefore valid and irreversible. Fourth, this could not be the case unless their consciences were illuminated by a divine and sufficient Light. Conscience is nothing more than the sense we have, or judgment we make, of our faithfulness to God's will—as God gives us an understanding of that will. To ensure only a true and scriptural use is made of this word 'conscience,' I limit it to judgments about our duty to live a virtuous and holy life. We cannot miss or dispute that the apostle evidently does the same (read Romans 2:7-9). Indeed, it was the judgment of conscience that guided the apostles in preaching the gospel and urging it on all people. The beloved disciple, calling it 'heart,' also holds it up as the judge of a person's present and future state: "If our hearts condemn us, God is greater than our hearts and knows everything; but if our hearts do not condemn us, we can be confident before God" (1 John 3:20-21). Plain and strong words! And what are they about? Just this: Do we love God in truth and in deed? And how do we show that? The answer: By keeping his commandments (John 14:15), which is simply living up to the duty we all know.

If anyone desires to further satisfy themselves of the divinity available to the Gentiles, let them read Plato, Seneca, Plutarch, Epictetus, Marcus Aurelius Antonius, and the Gentile writers. They will also find many of their sayings collected in the first part of a book called *The Christian Quaker.** There, they are compared with the testimony of Scripture, and their agreement with it is demonstrated. In these Gentile writings, they may find many excellent truths and taste great love of and devotion to virtue—a fruit that grows only on the Tree of Life in every age and in every nation.

Some of the most eminent early Christian writers, such as Justin Martyr, Origen, and Clemens Alexandrinus, had great respect for these Gentiles and did not fear that a defense of Christianity based on their works would harm Christianity's reputation. The early Christians used these sources to assist their followers in finding Truth, just as Paul did when he called on the Athenians to listen to the words of their own poets.†

---

* Penn's *The Christian Quaker* was published in 1674. It is available in a modern English translation in my *Twenty-First Century Penn* and online in the Earlham School of Religion's Digital Quaker Collection (http://dqc.esr.earlham.edu).

† The reference is to Paul's argument with the Athenians in Acts 17:16–34.

Chapter 7

The Various Dispensations of God

Bu, it may be asked, if there is only one Divine Principle, then why have there been so many different religions since the world began? The religions of the patriarchs (the Law of Moses) and of the early Christians have great differences— not to mention what has happened to Christianity since it was first introduced.

I cannot properly call religions 'different' if they claim the one, true God as their object of worship, whether that one God is called the only Savior, the Lord Jesus Christ, or the Light or Spirit of Christ, the agent and means of our conversion and eternal bliss. That would be like calling infant, child, and adult three persons rather than three stages in growth, or periods of time, in a single life. As was noted above, the various modes or ways in which God has appeared to different people have been appropriate to the various states of each of those people. In each case, it seems to have been God's primary purpose to prevent idolatry and depravity by directing their minds to the true object of worship and by encouraging virtue and holiness.

To the patriarchs, God added to their enlightenment by sending angels in the guise of travelers, and they in turn conveyed the message to their families. To the prophets, revelation came most often by the Holy Spirit when God sent them to preach to the Jews. In the gospel dispensation, the message was delivered by the Son—both externally in the flesh and internally by his spiritual appearance in the soul as the Light to the world. Yet all of these flowings of the Spirit, each suited to a particular people at a particular time, have sprung from the same source.

Truth Is the Same in All Forms

For your information and encouragement, remember that God's work with humanity is all of a single piece. In itself, that work has been sharply focused. In every dispensation, God's eye has been set on the same goal: to make us truly good by planting holy awe and reverence in our hearts. At times, our hardness of heart and darkness of mind were accommodated by spelling out the Holy Mind in ways that, to our more enlightened understanding, are simplistic and worldly. God has allowed Truth to put on various garments so it can better reach people in their lowly states and persuade them to give up false gods and wasted lives. At times, humanity has sunk far below the state that God intended for them, and people have become little more than brute beasts, forgetting their true strength and nobility.

Why Idolatry Abounds

Consider the prevalence of idolatry in earlier and darker times of the world, as described so well in the Scriptures. This is because idols are outward and visible, more sensual and attuned to please our senses than a more spiritual object of worship—and therefore seem more within the power of humanity (Genesis 31, 35; Exodus 20; Leviticus 21; Deuteronomy 29-32; Joshua 22-24). These gods, being the product of their followers' own hands, could not really help them. This was an argument that most galled their worshippers, and, for that reason, they were willing to ignore it. But still, the fact that it was outward and sensual—they could see the object of their devotion and address it whenever they wished—

gave it an advantage over true religion. In addition to being better suited to their dark and brutal state, it was often more fashionable.

Therefore, God, by many great afflictions and even greater deliverances, brought forth a people who might remember the hand that saved them and worship God only. God raised up the Jews in order to root out idolatry and plant the knowledge and love of God in their minds so they would be an example to all other nations. Anyone who reads Deuteronomy, which is a summary of the other four books of Moses,* cannot help but notice that good man's frequent and earnest care and concern for Israel on this very point. Nor can the reader miss how often—despite God's love, care, and patience for them—people slipped and lapsed into the idolatrous customs of the people around them. Numerous other Scriptures further inform us of this, especially in Isaiah 44-45, in Psalms 37 and 115, and in Jeremiah 10, where the people are proven wrong and rebuked by the Holy Spirit, who mocks their idols, treating them with holy disdain.

The Quakers' Testimony Is the Best Antidote: Walking by a Divine Principle

That which is furthest from idolatry, and the best antidote to it, is the Divine Principle we have proclaimed. The more people's minds are turned and brought to it, and the more they conform their faith, worship, and obedience to that Holy Illumination and Power, the nearer they grow to knowing the purpose of their creation and, consequently, to their Creator. They become more spiritually qualified and better able to worship God as God is—as we are told by our Lord Jesus Christ, a Spirit to be worshipped in Spirit and in Truth (John 4:24). This is the kind of worshippers

---

* According to tradition, Moses was the author of the first five books of the Bible: Genesis, Exodus, Leviticus, Numbers, and Deuteronomy.

God is calling in these gospel times. "The time is coming," Jesus said, "and is now here" (John 4:23). This is to say, "Some already do so, but more will." This is a plain assertion of the present time—a promise and prophesy of more true worshippers to come in the future. It makes clear the intended change away from ceremonial worship and an outward state of the church to a spiritual one. The clear meaning of this text is that the time is here and coming when worship will be more inward than outward—when worship will be more suited to the nature of God and to our own better selves and natures. Worship will be offered in Spirit and in Truth. 'In Spirit' means through the power of the Spirit. 'In Truth' means in reality—not in shadows, ceremonies, or forms—but in sincerity, with and in the Life, divinely prepared and enlivened. This enables us not only to offer right worship but also to enter into intimate communion and fellowship with God, who is a Spirit.

The Purpose of All God's Manifestations: That Humanity Might Be God's Image and Delight

If all is given its proper weight, it will be seen that God, in each manifestation, has come nearer and nearer to the innermost parts of humanity. In this way, God reaches into our understandings and opens our hearts, bringing us to a plainer and closer communion with Godself in the spirit. It is there that each of us must seek and find the knowledge of God for our eternal happiness.

All of creation testifies to the power and wisdom of God and to God's goodness toward humanity. Indeed, many point to creation as evidence for the existence of God, but above all else, it is humanity itself that is the proof. We are the precious stone in the ring, the most glorious jewel in the universe—the whole of which seems to have been made and dedicated to our reasonable use, service, and satisfaction. "But God's delight" (by whom, the Holy Spirit tells us, we were made) "is in the inhabited world, with the human race" (Proverbs 8:31) and with those that are "contrite in spirit" (Isaiah 66:1-2). And why are we God's delight? Because of all creation, only humanity is made in God's likeness (Genesis 1:26). This is how intimate humanity's relationship is to God, for of all creatures, only we have the honor of being in God's image. By this resemblance to God, I might say, came our kindred to God and our knowledge of God. Thus, the closest and best way for us to know and to truly understand God is to seek God's image within ourselves. As we find that, we will find God and know God.

We are God's image in two respects. The first is in our immortal nature. Second, that nature possesses qualities such as wisdom, justice, mercy, holiness, and patience (in a small way, proportional to our capacity) that are infinitely and incomparably to be found in our Creator. As we become more holy, just, merciful, and patient in ourselves, we will come to know the original by analogy—by observing the workmanship within ourselves, we can become acquainted with the Holy Workman.

This, Reader, is the regeneration and new creature that we urge. We say all ought to be religious and walk in this world according to this rule of peace and mercy (Galatians 6:15-16). As I have said, we share in two worlds. Our bodies are of this world; our souls are of the other world. The body is the temple of the soul, the soul is the temple of the Word, and the Word is the great temple and revelation of God. Through the body, the soul looks into and sees the physical world; through the Word, it can behold God and the world that is without end. Much more could be said about how God has ordered things and their respective qualities, but I must be brief.

Chapter 8

Satisfaction and Justification according to the Scriptures

Although we have many good things to say about how Christ appears in and works in the soul to awaken, convict, and convert it, some object that Quakers neglect the death and sufferings of Christ. Our adversaries say Quakers have little reverence for the doctrine of Christ's satisfaction to God for our sins and that we do not believe that the active and passive obedience of Christ, when he lived in the world, is the only basis for a sinner's justification before God.

The doctrines of Satisfaction and Justification, when truly understood, are so completely intertwined that each is the necessary consequence of the other. What we say about them is only what has the sanction of Scripture and what, for the most part, can be stated in words taken from the Bible. We believe that whenever any difficulty arises, whether from obscure language, mistranslation, or the dust stirred up by squabbles among partisan writers or overeducated critics, it is always best to stay as close as possible to the actual words of the text and to view anything else charitably.

I will first speak negatively, telling what we do not accept. Some, who are more hasty than wise, have used these things to accuse us of belittling the efficacy of the sufferings and death of Christ.

Notions We Cannot Believe

First, we cannot believe Christ is the cause of God's love. Rather we hold Christ is the effect of that love. John the beloved disciple testified to this in his third chapter, "God so loved the world that he gave his only Son, so that everyone who believes in him will not perish but have eternal life" (John 3:16).

Second, we reject the idea that God could use no other way to save sinners except by requiring the death and sufferings of his Son to satisfy his offended honor. Nor do we accept that Christ's death and sufferings were necessary and unavoidable to achieve satisfaction for the eternal death and misery that people deserved for their sin and transgression of the laws of God. These notions portray God's mercy as unconcerned about our salvation. Indeed, we stand too far from God's infinite wisdom and power to pretend we could ever judge whether God acted freely or out of necessity.

Third, we cannot say that Jesus Christ was the greatest sinner in the world because he bore our sins on his cross (1 Peter 2:24) or because he, who was sinless, was made to bear sin for us (2 Corinthians 5:21). This statement, though grossly insulting and scripturally unsound, is often spoken by great preachers and professors* of religion.

Fourth, we cannot believe Christ's death and sufferings so completely satisfy God or justify us that we are thereby accepted by God. Christ's acts indeed make it possible for people to be accepted by God, but it is only with the obedience of faith and the sanctification of the Spirit that they can attain and maintain that state of acceptance. We cannot imagine that a person would be

---

* A 'professor' was a person who professed or claimed belief in the tenets of a religion.

justified before God who stands self-condemned, that anyone can be in Christ who has not become a new creature (2 Corinthians 5:17), or that God would look upon anyone as anything but what they truly are. We term it a state of presumption, not a state of salvation, for anyone to call Jesus 'Lord' unless he or she is led to that declaration by the Holy Spirit; or 'Master' when he is not the master of their minds; or 'Savior' when they are not saved from sin by him; or 'Redeemer' when they are not redeemed from their passion, pride, covetousness, wantonness, vanity, arrogance, or the honors, friendships, and glories of this world. Those who do so deceive themselves because God will not be mocked. "They will reap what they sow" (Galatians 6:7). Even though Christ died for us, we must, with the assistance of his grace, "continue to work out our own salvation with fear and trembling" (Philippians 2:12). Just as he died for sin, we must die to sin. Otherwise, we cannot claim to be saved by the death and sufferings of Christ or to be thoroughly justified and accepted by God.

What has been said so far has been the negative. Now I will tell you what we claim and accept with regard to justification.

Christ, a Sacrifice and a Mediator

We do believe Jesus Christ was our holy sacrifice, atonement, and propitiation; he bore our iniquities, and by his wounds we are healed (Isaiah 53:5) of the wounds Adam and Eve gave us in their fall. We believe God is right to forgive those who are true penitents because of the holy offering Christ made of himself to God for us. We believe that what he did and suffered satisfied and pleased God and was offered for the sake of a fallen humanity that had displeased God. We believe that through the offering up of himself once for all (Hebrews 10:10), through the Eternal Spirit, he has forever perfected those in all times who are sanctified, those "who follow not their passions, but the Spirit" (Romans 8:1).

The Two Parts of Justification: From the Guilt of Sin and from Sin's Power and Pollution

In short, justification consists of two parts: justification from the guilt of sin and justification from the power and pollution of sin. In this sense, it provides clear and complete acceptance by God. Without the second part, many religiously inclined souls are left in doubt, conscience-ridden, and despondent despite all that their teachers have told them of the extent and effectiveness of the first part of justification. It is a source of widespread unhappiness among those who profess to be Christians that they have been too willing to hide their own active and passive disobedience under the cloak of Christ's active and passive obedience.

We reverently and humbly acknowledge that the first part of justification is the result only of the death and sufferings of Christ—nothing we can do ourselves, even by the work of the Holy Spirit, is sufficient to cancel our debts or wipe out old scores. It is the power and consequence of that propitiatory offering, if met with faith and repentance, that justifies us from the sins that are past. It is the power of Christ's Spirit in our hearts that purifies and makes us acceptable before God. Until our hearts have been purged of sin, God will not accept them. God rightly accuses, denounces, and condemns those who entertain sin in their hearts, and such people are not in a justified state. Condemnation and justification are in opposition—those who believe themselves to be justified by the active and passive obedience of Christ although they are not themselves actively and passively obedient to the Spirit of Christ Jesus are powerfully and dangerously deluded.

For crying out against this sin-pleasing notion (which we cannot call a doctrine), we are publicly scorned and denounced as deniers and despisers of the death and sufferings of our Lord Jesus Christ. But let those who walk unrighteously under that pretended justification know that they add to Christ's sufferings—they crucify afresh the Son of God and trample the blood of the covenant under their feet. "God will not acquit the guilty nor justify the disobedient and unfaithful" (Job 8:20).

These people deceive themselves, and, at the Great and Final Judgment, they will not hear, "Come you that are blessed" (Matthew 25:34); it cannot be said to them, "Well done, good and faithful servant" (Matthew 25:23). Rather, those who live and die in a contemptible and condemnable state will hear, "Depart from me, you who are cursed [etc.]" (Matthew 25:41).

Exhortation to the Reader

Therefore, O my Reader! rest not, thinking you are completely saved by what Christ has done for you in his blessed person without you, but strive to know his power and kingdom within you. The strong man, who has for too long lived within you, must be bound and his belongings removed (Mark 3:27), his works destroyed, and his sin ended. As 1 John 3:7 tells us, "Little children, let no one deceive you. Those that do righteousness are righteous." "To that end," says the beloved disciple, "Christ came so that all things may become new—new heavens and a new earth, in which righteousness dwells" (Revelation 21:5; see also 2 Peter 3:13). In this way, you will come to glorify God in your body and your spirit—both of which are God's—and live for God and not for yourself. Your love, joy, worship, and obedience—your very life and all you do in it—and your studies, meditations, and devotions will be spiritual. The Father and the Son will make their home in you (John 14:23) and Christ will reveal himself to you, for "the Lord confides in those who love and revere him" (Psalms 25:14). You will have a blessing or holy anointing that leads you into all Truth, and you will not need human teachings (John 16:13; 1 John 2:20, 27). You will be better taught, instructed directly by the Divine Oracle. You will not depend on hearsay or the words of traditional Christians but on a fresh and living witness from those who have seen with their own eyes, heard with their own ears, and touched with their own hands the Word of Life in all its works for their souls' salvation (1 John 1:1). In this Friends meet. In this they preach. In this they pray and praise.

Behold the New Covenant fulfilled—the church and worship of Christ, the great anointed of God, and the great anointing of God—in God's Holy Priesthood and in the work of God's church!

Chapter 9

Belief in Christ and in His Work, Both in His Doings and in His Sufferings

Some say Quakers are ambiguous in what we profess regarding Christ's coming in the flesh or that we allegorize that event so as to mean only our own flesh. Some say that whenever we mention Christ, we mean only a mystery or some mystical sense of him, whether we are speaking of his coming, birth, miracles, sufferings, death, resurrection, ascension, mediation, or judgment.

To eliminate any misunderstanding among those who may be like-minded, and to inform and reclaim for Christ those who are under the power and prejudice of our attackers, let me speak plainly: We do religiously believe and confess—to the glory of God the Father and the honor of his dear and beloved Son—that Jesus Christ took our nature on himself (Hebrews 2:17) and was like us in all things excepting sin (Hebrews 4:15); and that he was born of the virgin Mary, suffered under Pontius Pilate, the Roman governor, was crucified, died, and was buried in the sepulcher of Joseph of Arimathea. He rose again on the third day and ascended into heaven, where he sits at the right hand of God, in the power and majesty of his Father. One day, the world will be judged by that blessed man, Christ Jesus—each according to his or her own deeds.

Our Belief in and Testimony of Christ's Inward and Spiritual Appearance in the Soul

Because we believe all this, must not we also believe the rest that Christ said? "He that is with you will be in you" (John 14:17). "I in them and they in me" (John 17:23). "When God was pleased to reveal his Son in me . . ." (Galatians 1:15-16). "The mystery that has been hidden for ages is Christ among the Gentiles, Christ within you, the hope of glory" (Colossians 1:26-27). "Unless you have failed the test, Christ is within you!" (2 Corinthians 13:5) Or are we to be misrepresented as denying Christ in the flesh and the holy purpose of his taking it—in each particular of his work and suffering—because we believe and urgently preach the necessity that others believe, receive, and obey Christ's inward and spiritual appearance and manifestation? Is it because we preach that his Light, Grace, and Spirit in the hearts and consciences of men and women can expose, convict, convert, and reform them? This is cruel and unrighteous treatment! Nor would our harsh and heated adversaries accept such treatment from others—to do to others as you would have them do to you is too often not part of their practice, regardless of what they preach.

It Is Impossible to Be Saved by Christ While Rejecting His Work and Power within Us

Moreover, we declare to the whole world that we cannot expect men and women to be saved by their belief in one form of justification without knowing and living the other. That is what we oppose, not the Blessed Manifestation of Christ in the flesh. We say Christ overcame our common enemy, defeated him in the open field, and in our nature conquered the one who had overcome and triumphed over Adam and Eve and all their descendants. Just as Christ himself overcame that one in our nature, so he overcomes the enemy within us when we receive and obey his divine grace. Christ by his Light in our consciences reveals the enemy and enables us to resist him and all his fiery darts (Ephesians 6:16), to fight the good fight of faith, to overcome him ourselves, and to lay claim to eternal life (1 Timothy 6:12).

The Dispensation of Grace: Its Nature and Extent

This is the Dispensation of Grace, which we declare has in one degree or another come to all, teaching those who will receive it "to renounce ungodliness and worldly passions and to live self-controlled, upright, and godly lives in this world while we wait for the blessed hope (which no one else can justly do) and the glorious appearance of our great God and Savior Jesus Christ" (Titus 2:11-13). We minister to others from the teaching, experience, and direction of this grace with the goal of turning people's minds to that grace in themselves so all will be doing "the good and pleasing will of God" (Romans 12:2), "working out their salvation with fear and trembling" (Philippians 2:12), and "confirming their high and heavenly calling and election" (2 Peter 1:10). No one else can do that, no matter what religion they profess, which church they attend, or the quality of their personal character, because "you will reap what you sow" (Galatians 6:7) and "you are the servant of the one you obey" (Romans 6:16). We cannot be children of God and heirs of eternal glory if we are not regenerated. To be born again, another Spirit and Principle must win over, transform, instruct, and govern us—not the spirit of this world or our own depraved spirits (1 Corinthians 2:12) but only the Spirit that lived in Christ. Unless that Spirit lives within us, we cannot be Christ's (Romans 8:9). This Spirit begins by awaking the soul to its sin, and it ends in conversion and perseverance. One follows the other, with conversion being the consequence of an awakening that is accepted and perseverance being the natural fruit of conversion and of being born of God. These "do not sin, because God's seed lives within them" (1 John 3:9). They who are faithful to the end receive what was promised (Hebrews 6:15), which is everlasting life.

Acknowledgment of the Death and Sufferings of Christ

Let my readers take this with them. We do acknowledge that Christ, through his holy works and sufferings ("being a Son, he learned obedience," Hebrews 5:8), has obtained his Father's mercy for mankind. His obedience affects every piece and part of our salvation since in it he became a conqueror and held even captivity as a captive (Ephesians 4:8) and obtained gifts for all—great and precious promises—that by them we might first escape the corruptions of the world caused by evil desires and become participants in the divine nature (2 Peter 1:4). We do believe and confess that the active and passive obedience of Christ Jesus has brought about our salvation from the power and pollution of sin as well as from the guilt of sin. He has given this gift to all so they may see their transgressions and sinfulness, so they can repent and turn away from them, and so they will sin and transgress no more. By this gift, they will each day depend on God for the strength to resist the fiery darts of the enemy and find comfort in the obedience of faith in and faithfulness to the leading of this divine grace from the Son of God.

Christ is both a conqueror and a sacrifice through suffering, and those who reject the divine gift he obtained in this way do not please God and do not truly believe in God, nor are they truly

Christians or truly saved. "Woman," said Christ to the Samaritan at the well, "If you knew the gift of God and who it is that speaks to you . . ." (John 4:10). People do not know Christ or God, "who to know is life eternal" (John 17:3), because they are ignorant of the gift of God, which is that "each will receive a share in the Spirit of God for the common good" (1 Corinthians 12:7)—it is this that reveals Christ and God to the soul (1 Corinthians 2:10).

Flesh and blood alone cannot reveal Christ and God. Oxford and Cambridge cannot do it. Learning languages and philosophy cannot do it. Those who do not know God by God's Wisdom take these things for their wisdom (1 Corinthians 1:21). Although they are clear, careful, and correct in their understandings of those things, alas, it is all in vain and misguided. Because they put their trust in these things and seek God there, they fall further and further from the inward and saving knowledge of God.

The key of David is quite another thing: "What it shuts, no one can open; what it opens, no one can shut" (Revelation 3:7). All who receive and accept the gift of God into their hearts have this key. It opens to them the knowledge of God and of themselves. It gives them new senses of sight and taste and a new way of understanding things that education and traditional knowledge cannot provide. This is the beginning of God's new creation; through it we come to be new beings.

We boldly declare there is no other way than this one for people to come into Christ, to be true Christians, or to receive the advantages that come from the death and sufferings of the Lord Jesus Christ. Therefore, on the authority of our own experience as well as of Scripture, we say that Christ is not a saving sacrifice for any who refuse to follow his example. Those who reject the gift deny the giver—instead of denying their own desires for the giver's sake.

Oh, if only people were wise! If they would just consider the end they are approaching and what is required for that end to be a peaceful one! Why should they die clutching vain hopes for eternal life while death reigns in their hearts? Why do they anticipate a future life with God but do not live up to him or walk with him in this one!

Awake, you who sleep in sin! Awake, you who rest in self-righteousness! Christ will give you Life! Only he is "the Lord from heaven, the life-giving Spirit" (1 Corinthians 15:45, 47), and we can receive that Life if we do not resist his Spirit or reject it by disobedience.

Receive, love, and obey all the holy leadings and teachings of Christ's Spirit (Romans 8:14-15)! To that Holy Spirit, I entrust my readers so they can better see where they truly are and come to have true belief in and take full advantage of the works and sufferings of our Dear and Blessed Lord and Savior Jesus Christ. From the power and pollution of sin (as well as from its guilt), he saves all who hear his knock and open the door of their hearts to him (Revelation 3:20) so he can come in and bring about real and thorough reformation in them and for them. Only in this way can the real benefit, power, and effect of his works and sufferings come into our lives and let us know, according to the doctrine of the apostle, fellowship with Christ in his sufferings and death (Philippians 3:10). Those who live in sin do not know this spiritual communion, though they claim to be saved by that death and those sufferings. Much more might be said about this matter, but I must be brief.

Our Adversaries' Unreasonableness

To conclude this chapter, we are not surprised that we are misunderstood, misconstrued, and misrepresented in what we believe and what we do to achieve salvation—better people than us were so treated in primitive times. Nor is it only our religious doctrines—our practices in worship and discipline have been mishandled in similar ways. What I sincerely desire, no matter how unfairly people treat us, is that they not deceive themselves with respect to their own salvation. Although they seem to credit Christ with everything, they risk being discredited by him on the last day. Read the seventh chapter of Matthew's gospel: Everyone who hears Christ, the Word of God, and does what he commands, following his blessed example, is a wise builder. They have positioned their house well and built with good materials. When the last shock and judgment comes, that house will stand (Matthew 7:24-25).

For this reason, we are often plain, direct, and serious with people: Christ did not come to save you *in* your sins but *from* them! Do not believe Christ has done it all for you—that you are released from his yoke and burden (Matthew 11:29-30), from his cross and example. If he has changed nothing within you and you have given up nothing for the love of him, you will awaken in dreadful surprise at the sound of the last trumpet and hear this sad and irrevocable sentence: "Depart from me, you evildoers, I do not know you!" (Matthew 7:23)

All may yet avoid that terrible end by attending to Wisdom's voice, turning at her reproach, following her in the ways of righteousness and along the paths of justice so their souls will inherit the substance, the riches, and righteousness of the kingdom of the Father (Proverbs 1:20, 23; 8:20-21).

Chapter 10

The True Worship of God

As the Lord, by divine grace, worked in the hearts of God's people, he led them to a divine worship and ministry. They came to experience Christ's words, "God is a Spirit, and his worshippers must worship in Spirit and Truth." These are the kind of worshippers the Father seeks (John 4:23-24). They accept what the Spirit has revealed in them. By it, they were taught to give up that which is evil and to do that which is good in their daily lives (3 John 1:11). When they gather, they sit down and wait for the Holy Spirit, both to let them see their spiritual states and conditions before God and to direct them in proper worship. As they became aware of their shortcomings and spiritual infirmities, in the secret of their hearts, prayer would spring to God through Jesus Christ for help, assistance, and sustenance. They dare not "awake their beloved too soon" (Song of Solomon 8:4), nor "approach the throne of the King of Glory until the scepter was extended to them" (Esther 4:11), nor "worry what they would say" (Luke 12:11), nor carefully choose words of their own, nor adopt another's careful forms and phrases. To pray in any way not led by the Spirit would be offering God an unholy fire (Leviticus 10:1). It is like asking for something, but not in the name and power of our Lord Jesus Christ, who prayed and spoke as a person with authority (Matthew 7:29)—with the power and strength to reach and pierce the heavens. This authority is granted to all who obey his Light, Grace, and Spirit in their solemn waiting on him. It is the Quakers' principle that fire must come from heaven (1 Chronicles 21:26). Life and power must come from above if the soul is to acceptably pour itself out before God.

Only when a coal from God's holy altar touches our lips (Isaiah 6:6-7) can we pray and praise as we ought to. This principle, drawn from Scripture, is our experience and our practice. Blessed be God! Because of this principle, we have turned away from all human forms of worship. These are not based on the direction, instruction, and assistance of the Spirit of Christ but on human times, designs, and forms. It is not our own wills or desires that lead us to worship as we do but the will of the One who has called us and brought us into God's own spiritual worship. We are who we are out of obedience to God.

True Ministry by Inspiration

Just as our worship is based on the workings of the Spirit and of Truth within us, so too is our ministry. The Holy Testimonies of the servants of God have always been directed by the workings of his blessed Spirit, and so they must be today. Ministry that does not drink from the spring of the Spirit of Christ is merely from the speaker, not from Christ. Christian ministers are called to deliver what they receive—this is the teaching of Scripture. What we receive is not our own, much less another person's, but the Lord's. Not only do we not steal the thoughts of our neighbors, we also do not prepare nor speak our own words. And, if we are not to prepare what we are to say on our own behalf before a judge (Matthew 10:19), then we ought not to prepare what we are to say for and from God before other people. We are called to minister as the oracles of God (1 Peter 4:11). To do so, we must receive the words of ministry from Christ, God's great oracle. If we are to speak only what we receive, then we must put aside all we study, collect, and create in our own minds because that does not come from the mind of Christ but from our own imaginings and will not benefit the people.

Plain Scriptural Support

In the fourteenth chapter of his first Epistle to the Corinthians, the Apostle Paul commended all to speak and all to prophesy as they were moved or as anything was revealed to them by the Spirit for the edification of the church (1 Corinthians 14:3, 6, 31). That is, all may preach what is revealed to them, as the Spirit gives them the words, to instruct and benefit others. And if the Spirit must give Christ's ministers their words, then those who belong to the Spirit must be careful not to say anything beyond what they have received. A consequence of this is that those who go beyond their guide and speak without waiting for the words of the Spirit are easily seen as not being among Christ's ministers. They run where God has not sent them and cannot benefit the people. Indeed, how could they? It is impossible for ordinary people, no matter their learning or degrees or artful style, to "turn people from darkness to Light and from the power of Satan to God" (Acts 26:18). That is the purpose of gospel ministry, and only those who are inspired—gifted by God, taught and directed by God's heavenly Spirit—can be qualified for so great, so inward, and so spiritual a work.

Christ's Ministers Are True Witnesses, Speaking from Experience

The ministers of Christ are his witnesses, and witnesses are valuable for their ability to report what they themselves have heard, seen, or touched. Thus, the beloved disciple states the truth and authority for their mission and ministry in his first epistle: "That which we have heard, which we have seen with our eyes, which we have looked at and our hands have touched—this we proclaim to you, so you also may have fellowship with us. And our fellowship is with the Father and with his Son, Jesus Christ" (1 John 1:1, 3). If Christ's ministers are his witnesses, then they must know for themselves what they preach about. They must have fully experienced the spiritual states and conditions they describe and know directly those truths they declare—otherwise, they have not come in through the door but over the wall and are thieves and robbers (John 10:1-2). Those with the key of David come in through the door, which is Christ Jesus (John 10:7). Christ acknowledges and approves them. They have been anointed by the one high priest of the gospel dispensation (Hebrews 3:1), who breathes on them and lays his hands on them. He anoints and strengthens them for their journey. He renews their horns with oil* so they are pure and fresh for every task and every occasion to which he calls them or in which he places them.

Free Ministry Is the Mark of Christ's Ministers

Nor is this all—true ministers receive without payment and give without compensation (Matthew 10:8). They do not teach for a salary, prophesy for money, or preach for gifts and rewards. It was Christ's holy command to his ministers to give freely, and that is our practice. Truly, we cannot help but be amazed that our ministry has been reviled but preaching for pay is not. Indeed, that is the mark of a false prophet, and that has been frequently and severely condemned by the true prophets of God (Micah 3:11). I do not wish to be uncharitable, but do the guilty remember who it was that offered Peter and John money to be made a minister so

---

* David and Solomon were anointed as kings of Israel with a horn of oil (1 Samuel 16:13, 1 Kings 1:39).

he could make a living at it? And what Peter's answer was (Acts 8:18-20)?

We pray the Lord will touch the hearts of those who pay to become ministers and who make a living as a preacher so they will see what ground they are building on. We pray they will repent and turn to the Lord, receiving God's mercy and becoming living witnesses to God's power and goodness in their souls. They may then be able to tell others what God has done for them—this is the root and ground of true ministry, and God will bless it.

I could say much more on this subject, but what I have already said is sufficient for now, except for this: I cannot help but notice that when a religion lures people with lucre to entice them to ministry, there is great danger they will run faster to that calling than is good for a true gospel minister.

An Objection Answered

It has been suggested that our form of ministry and worship might make some people careless and promote spiritual pride in others. May it not cause great mischief and false or perverted religion?

By no means! When people come of age, they have a right to receive their inheritance. Our words are designed to bring people to the great Word. Then the promise of God will be fulfilled: "All will be taught by the LORD, from the least to the greatest. In righteousness they will be established, and great will be their peace" (Isaiah 54:13-14). To these words of the evangelical prophet, the beloved disciple (providing a full answer to this objection) adds: "I am writing to you about those who are trying to lead you astray. The anointing you received remains in you. You do not need anyone to teach you—this anointing teaches you all things. It is true and not a lie. As it has taught you, abide in him" (1 John 2:26-27).

There are three things to be noted in this passage. First, this epistle was written under extraordinary circumstances in order to prevent the apostle's readers from being deluded. Second, he acknowledges a closer and superior minister than himself—the Anointing or Grace they had received—not only for the immediate situation but for all cases and all times. Third, if his readers only followed its instruction, they would have no need for any earthly directions. Nor should they fear they could be led astray by any ministry not inspired by the power of that anointing (indeed, I believe the truest meaning of this message is that those who are faithful should have no fear). Look also to Paul's Epistle to the Thessalonians, "Concerning love among you, you do not need me to write to you, for you yourselves have been taught by God to love one another" (1 Thessalonians 4:9). Even so, a little help is sometimes useful and can be a great blessing if it comes from God—such was John the Baptist's message when he pointed all to Christ, "Behold the Lamb of God! I baptize you with water, but he will baptize you with the Holy Spirit and with fire" (John 1:29, 33). This is what true ministry does! When people are wrapped up in their day-to-day concerns and lost in the shadows cast by sin and Satan, God is pleased to send enlightening servants to awaken them and turn them from the darkness to the Light within themselves. Through obedience to that Light, they can become children of the Light (John 12:36), find fellowship with one another in it (1 John 1:7) and, in the end, share the inheritance of the saints in the Light forever (Colossians 1:12).

This is the way God has chosen to call and gather people. A living and holy ministry is of great advantage in watching over and strengthening the young. It comforts and protects the weak and simple-minded. But still, the more inward the ministry is, the more people will come to be taught directly by God—by the Light of God's Word and Spirit in their hearts—and the less need they will have for outward ministry. Read Isaiah 60:19-20, which all agree is a gospel promise: "The sun will no more be your light by day, nor will the brightness of the moon shine on you, for the Lord will be your everlasting light, and your God will be your glory. Your sun will never set again, and your moon will wane no more; the Lord will be your everlasting light, and your days of sorrow will end." The references to sun and moon are generally understood to mean the outward practices of the church. Compare this passage with John 1:13; Romans 1:19; 1 Corinthians 2:11, 15; 1 Thessalonians 4:9; 1 John 2:20, 27; and Revelation 21:22-24. All of these passages demonstrate the complete sufficiency and glorious advantages of the inward and spiritual teachings that we assert. It is certain that as people grow in grace and come to feel the anointing of the Spirit within themselves, the action of the Holy Spirit will be less as words (although it may be felt as words) and more as sharing directly in the Life of the Holy Spirit. Then their preaching will turn increasingly to praise; their worship will more and more walk with, rather than talk of, God. That is worship in Truth—bowing to God's will at all times and in all places—the purest and truest worship that people in this world can offer. By conforming to God's will as it is revealed by the Light in our hearts, we achieve communion with God and with each other. Without obedience to that will and faithfulness to God's Word, there is no fellowship with God, no Light from the face of God to be enjoyed, and no peace or assurance of salvation.

I have called this the purest and truest state of worship. Contrast it with the customary days and places and all the accompanying solemnity that were the mark of the old covenant and dispensation. Altars, ark and temples, Sabbaths and festivals, etc. are not to be found in the writings of the New Testament! As Paul wrote, every day is alike and every place the same—all must be dedicated to the Lord (Romans 14:5-8, 17; 1 Corinthians 8:6; Colossians 2:16-17). He directed our attention to a state beyond this world, saying, "To live is Christ and to die is gain" (Philippians 1:21). The life he lived was "the faith of the Son of God and therefore it was not Paul who lived, but Christ who lived in him" (Galatians 2:20)—Christ ruled, directed, and guided him. That is the true Christian life—a life that rises above the body and its senses, a life of conversion and regeneration to which all God's dispensations and the ministries of all God's servants have pointed. This is the goal of God's work with humanity. Here everyone is a temple and every family a church. Every place is a meeting place and every visit an opportunity for worship. Wait just a little while and you will see it coming more and more. Even now, the Lord is preparing a people to enter into this Sabbath, this state of rest.

But do not think we undervalue public and solemn meetings— we hold them all over the nation, wherever the Lord has called us. Even if there are only two or three in a corner of a country, we meet as the apostle urged the saints of his time and as he condemned those who neglected to assemble (Hebrews 10:25). What we are showing you, dear Reader, is simply a better way to worship. Many go to those public meetings and come away still governed by their human nature—spiritually, they are dead and dry. But worshippers in Spirit and Truth, whose hearts bow to the will of God and whose minds adore the eternal God, are the true, acceptable, constant, and living worshippers—whether in meetings or out of them. They know God, who is a Spirit, in and by that Spirit. They conform to God's will and walk with God in a spiritual life. For them, all outward assemblies are a great comfort, and so they meet for public testimony of religion and worship, for the education and encouragement of those who are still young in the Truth, and to call and gather others (who are now going astray) to the knowledge of that Truth. Blessed be God! That work is not in vain—by it, many are added to the church that we hope and believe will be saved (Acts 2:47).

Chapter 11

Against Tithes

Since God has called us away from a human ministry, we cannot in good conscience do anything to support and sustain such a ministry. For that reason, and not because we are greedy or grasping, we refuse to pay tithes or any similar so-called obligations. Many books have been written about this matter in our defense. We simply cannot support what we cannot approve and what we testify against. If we did so, we would contradict ourselves.

Against All Swearing

We do not dare to swear because Christ forbids it—"I tell you: Do not swear at all . . . but let your Yes be Yes, and your No, No" (Matthew 5:34, 37)—and James, a true disciple, affirms, "Above all, my beloved, do not swear, either by heaven or by earth or by any other oath, but let your 'Yes' be yes and your 'No' be no" (James 5:12). To swear is not only unnecessary but evil. The reason to require the swearing of oaths is that some lie. It was thought that swearing would frighten liars into telling the truth and assure others that what they heard under oath was true, but for the true Christian, Yes is Yes and there is no need for an oath to ensure it. Such use, therefore, is unnecessary and superfluous and comes only from evil. This is what James taught, what the primitive

Christians practiced, and, as can be seen in the *Book of Martyrs*,* what the earliest and best of the Protestant reformers followed.

Against All War among Christians

We also believe war ought to cease among the followers of the Lamb, Christ Jesus, who taught his disciples to forgive and love their enemies, not to fight against and kill them. The weapons of Christ's true followers are not physical but spiritual, made mighty by God to destroy sin and wickedness and to overthrow the author of sin (2 Corinthians 10:3-4). Not only is this the most Christian way, it is also the most rational—love and persuasion have more force than the weapons of war. Even the worst of humanity cannot easily bring themselves to harm those that they really think love them. In the end, love and patience must have the victory.

Against the Greetings of the Times

We dare not offer worldly honor or use the frequent and fashionable greetings of these times. We see plainly these are signs of vanity, pride, and pretentiousness. Christ also forbade them in his day (Luke 10:4) and called the love of them a sign of decline from the simplicity of purer times (Mark 12:38). His disciples and their followers were observed to obey their Master's decree. We do not do this to set ourselves apart from others or out of pride, poor manners, or spite but in obedience to the sight and sense we have received from the Spirit of Christ of the evil in it.

---

* John Foxe (1516-1587) published *A History of the Lives, Sufferings and Triumphant Deaths of the Early Christian and the Protestant Martyrs* in 1554. Of particular importance to William Penn and his readers were the extensive descriptions of the persecution and martyrdom of English Protestants during the reign of Queen Mary (1553-1558).

For Plainness in Speech

For the same reason, we have returned to the original plainness in our speech, using 'thou' and 'thee' when referring to a single person.* Although people will say nothing else when speaking to God, they can hardly endure it when they hear it from us. It has been a great trial to their pride and has revealed the spiritual blindness and weakness of many. Whatever people may think or say about us, we do this purely for conscience's sake. We may be despised, and certainly have been badly treated for it, but because of it we are now better known and others are better informed. In short, both Scripture and grammar direct us to this practice, and we are at peace with ourselves in obeying.

Against Mixed Marriages

We cannot allow mixed marriage, which is to join with any who are not of the Society of Friends. We oppose and disown any of our members who reject this rule and enter into such a marriage. They can be restored to membership if they sincerely repent—we do not ask them to divorce. This topic is covered more completely and directly in my book *The Rise & Progress of the People Called Quakers*.†

---

* In the mid-seventeenth century, Standard English employed different singular and plural forms of the second-person pronoun. The convention of the time was to show respect to an individual of higher social standing by using the plural forms of address. Plural forms were also sometimes used as a blatant form of flattery. Friends believed these practices fed false pride in the recipient and insisted on always using the singular forms when referring to a single person.

† Penn's *The Rise and Progress of the People Called Quakers* was published in 1694. It is available in a modern English translation in my *Twenty-First Century Penn* and online in the Earlham School of Religion's Digital Quaker Collection (http://dqc.esr.earlham.edu).

For Plainness in Apparel and Furnishings and No Sports and Pastimes after the Manner of This World

Plainness in dress and furniture is another testimony in which we are alone in the degree we practice it. Just as we use few words when we speak but stand by each one, likewise, we are temperate in our food and abstain from the recreations and pastimes of the world. This, the Spirit of our Lord Jesus Christ has taught us, is required of those who wish to be godly. "Let your moderation be known, for the Lord is near" (Philippians 4:5)—God is near to see and to judge every overindulgence or excess. We hope in this we have not given a bad example or caused any scandal.

On Observing Selected Days

We cannot in conscience observe the so-called holy days, public fasts, or feasts. These were invented and instituted by humanity, not by God; they are the products of a human will, not of a divine command.

On Public Behavior, the Care of the Poor, Marriage, and Maintaining Good Order in Our Society

Lastly, we have been led by this good Spirit of our Lord Jesus Christ (which is the subject of this discourse) to follow the example of the primitive Christians in exercising due care for one another. For the preservation of the whole Society of Friends, we call on all to behave in ways that are consistent with their professed beliefs.

First, with respect to our behavior both toward those within and those outside our society, we are called to act blamelessly—to be careful in our dealings with the world and faithful in our dealings with each other.

Second, we take up collections to meet the needs of the poor so that widows, orphans, and the helpless are cared for. We offer advice and counsel as well as material things.

Third, all within our religious society who intend to marry are required first to declare their intentions to and seek the approval of their parents or guardians—even before they propose it to one another—and only then to bring their request to their meeting. The meeting to which they belong is careful to determine whether they are clear to marry and, if so, allows them to solemnize their marriage in a public meeting called for that purpose. By these procedures, we prevent all secret or fraudulent marriages among us.

Fourth, and with the aim of maintaining good order, comforting and instructing all within the society, and keeping us in the ways of truth, meetings of our members are called to provide care and conduct business. These are held monthly in each district, quarterly within each region, and yearly for the whole nation to ensure accurate communications with each other on those things that sustain us in piety and charity.

By God's grace, we have been called to be a people, giving praise through God's beloved Son, our ever-blessed and only Redeemer, Jesus Christ, now and forever. Amen.

————————ooo————————

Thus, Reader, you can see the character of the people called Quakers in their doctrine, worship, ministry, practice, and discipline. Compare this to what you have read with Scripture and the example of the primitive church; we hope you will find this short discourse has lived up to its title: *Primitive Christianity Revived in the Faith & Practice of the People Called Quakers.*

Appendix
Bible Verses Cited

Note: All verses cited here are from the King James Version of the Bible. Sequential verses are combined if that is the only way they are cited in the text.

Genesis

1:3 And God said, Let there be light: and there was light.

1:26 And God said, Let us make man in our image, after our likeness: and let them have dominion over the fish of the sea, and over the fowl of the air, and over the cattle, and over all the earth, and over every creeping thing that creepeth upon the earth.

6:3 And the LORD said, My spirit shall not always strive with man, for that he also *is* flesh: yet his days shall be an hundred and twenty years

49:10 The sceptre shall not depart from Judah, nor a lawgiver from between his feet, until Shiloh come; and unto him *shall* the gathering of the people *be*.

Leviticus

10:1 And Nadab and Abihu, the sons of Aaron, took either of them his censer, and put fire therein, and put incense thereon, and offered strange fire before the LORD, which he commanded them not.

Deuteronomy

18:15 The LORD thy God will raise up unto thee a Prophet from the midst of thee, of thy brethren, like unto me; unto him ye shall hearken.

18:18 I will raise them up a Prophet from among their brethren, like unto thee, and will put my words in his mouth; and he shall speak unto them all that I shall command him.

30:12-14 It *is* not in heaven, that thou shouldest say, Who shall go up for us to heaven, and bring it unto us, that we may hear it, and do it? Neither *is* it beyond the sea, that thou shouldest say, Who shall go over the sea for us, and bring it unto us, that we may hear it, and do it? But the word *is* very nigh unto thee, in thy mouth, and in thy heart, that thou mayest do it.

First Samuel

16:13 Then Samuel took the horn of oil, and anointed him in the midst of his brethren: and the Spirit of the LORD came upon David from that day forward. So Samuel rose up, and went to Ramah.

First Kings

1:39 And Zadok the priest took an horn of oil out of the tabernacle, and anointed Solomon. And they blew the trumpet; and all the people said, God save king Solomon.

First Chronicles

21:26 And David built there an altar unto the LORD, and offered burnt offerings and peace offerings, and called upon the LORD; and he answered him from heaven by fire upon the altar of burnt offering.

Nehemiah

9:30 Yet many years didst thou forbear them, and testifiedst against them by thy spirit in thy prophets: yet would they not give ear: therefore gavest thou them into the hand of the people of the lands

Esther

4:11 All the king's servants, and the people of the king's provinces, do know, that whosoever, whether man or woman, shall come unto the king into the inner court, who is not called, *there is* one law of his to put *him* to death, except such to whom the king shall hold out the golden sceptre, that he may live: but I have not been called to come in unto the king these thirty days.

Job

8:20 Behold, God will not cast away a perfect *man*, neither will he help the evil doers.

18:5-6 Yea, the light of the wicked shall be put out, and the spark of his fire shall not shine. The light shall be dark in his tabernacle, and his candle shall be put out with him.

21:17 How oft is the candle of the wicked put out! and *how oft* cometh their destruction upon them! *God* distributeth sorrows in his anger.

24:13 They are of those that rebel against the light; they know not the ways thereof, nor abide in the paths thereof.

25:3 Is there any number of his armies? and upon whom doth not his light arise?

32:8 But *there is* a spirit in man: and the inspiration of the Almighty giveth them understanding.

38:15 And from the wicked their light is withholden, and the high arm shall be broken.

Psalms

18:28 For thou wilt light my candle: the LORD my God will enlighten my darkness.

25:14 The secret of the LORD *is* with them that fear him; and he will shew them his covenant.

27:1 The LORD *is* my light and my salvation; whom shall I fear? the LORD *is* the strength of my life; of whom shall I be afraid?

34:5 They looked unto him, and were lightened: and their faces were not ashamed.

36:9 For with thee *is* the fountain of life: in thy light shall we see light.

43:3 O send out thy light and thy truth: let them lead me; let them bring me unto thy holy hill, and to thy tabernacles.

51:6 Behold, thou desirest truth in the inward parts: and in the hidden part thou shalt make me to know wisdom.

118:27 God *is* the LORD, which hath shewed us light: bind the sacrifice with cords, *even* unto the horns of the altar.

119:105 Thy word *is* a lamp unto my feet, and a light unto my path.

119:10 With my whole heart have I sought thee: O let me not wander from thy commandments.

139:7 Whither shall I go from thy spirit? or whither shall I flee from thy presence?

139:8-10 If I ascend up into heaven, thou *art* there: if I make my bed in hell, behold, thou *art there. If* I take the wings of the morning, *and* dwell in the uttermost parts of the sea; Even there shall thy hand lead me, and thy right hand shall hold me

Proverbs

1:20-23 Wisdom crieth without; she uttereth her voice in the streets: She crieth in the chief place of concourse, in the openings of the gates: in the city she uttereth her words, *saying,*

How long, ye simple ones, will ye love simplicity? and the scorners delight in their scorning, and fools hate knowledge? Turn you at my reproof: behold, I will pour out my spirit unto you, I will make known my words unto you.

3:17 Her ways *are* ways of pleasantness, and all her paths *are* peace.

4:18 But the path of the just *is* as the shining light, that shineth more and more unto the perfect day.

6:22 When thou goest, it shall lead thee; when thou sleepest, it shall keep thee; and *when* thou awakest, it shall talk with thee.

8:1-4 Doth not wisdom cry? and understanding put forth her voice? She standeth in the top of high places, by the way in the places of the paths. She crieth at the gates, at the entry of the city, at the coming in at the doors. Unto you, O men, I call; and my voice *is* to the sons of man.

8:20-21 I lead in the way of righteousness, in the midst of the paths of judgment: That I may cause those that love me to inherit substance; and I will fill their treasures.

8:31 Rejoicing in the habitable part of his earth; and my delights *were* with the sons of men

13:9 The light of the righteous rejoiceth: but the lamp of the wicked shall be put out.

20:20 Whoso curseth his father or his mother, his lamp shall be put out in obscure darkness.

20:27 The spirit of man *is* the candle of the LORD, searching all the inward parts of the belly.

24:20 For there shall be no reward to the evil *man*; the candle of the wicked shall be put out.

Song of Solomon

8:4 I charge you, O daughters of Jerusalem, that ye stir not up, nor awake *my* love, until he please.

Isaiah

2:5 O house of Jacob, come ye, and let us walk in the light of the LORD.

6:6-7 Then flew one of the seraphims unto me, having a live coal in his hand, *which* he had taken with the tongs from off the altar: And he laid *it* upon my mouth, and said, Lo, this hath touched thy lips; and thine iniquity is taken away, and thy sin purged.

8:20 To the law and to the testimony: if they speak not according to this word, *it is* because *there is* no light in them.

26:2 Open ye the gates, that the righteous nation which keepeth the truth may enter in.

42:6 I the LORD have called thee in righteousness, and will hold thine hand, and will keep thee, and give thee for a covenant of the people, for a light of the Gentiles.

43:2 When thou passest through the waters, I *will be* with thee; and through the rivers, they shall not overflow thee: when thou walkest through the fire, thou shalt not be burned; neither shall the flame kindle upon thee.

44:24 Thus saith the LORD, thy redeemer, and he that formed thee from the womb, I *am* the LORD that maketh all *things*; that stretcheth forth the heavens alone; that spreadeth abroad the earth by myself.

49:6 And he said, It is a light thing that thou shouldest be my servant to raise up the tribes of Jacob, and to restore the preserved of Israel: I will also give thee for a light to the Gentiles, that thou mayest be my salvation unto the end of the earth.

53:5 But he *was* wounded for our transgressions, *he was* bruised for our iniquities: the chastisement of our peace *was* upon him; and with his stripes we are healed.

54:5 For thy Maker *is* thine husband; the LORD of hosts *is* his name; and thy Redeemer the Holy One of Israel; The God of the whole earth shall he be called.

54:13-14 And all thy children *shall be* taught of the LORD; and great *shall be* the peace of thy children. In righteousness shalt thou be established: thou shalt be far from oppression; for thou shalt not fear: and from terror; for it shall not come near thee.

60:19-20 The sun shall be no more thy light by day; neither for brightness shall the moon give light unto thee: but the LORD shall be unto thee an everlasting light, and thy God thy glory. Thy sun shall no more go down; neither shall thy moon withdraw itself: for the LORD shall be thine everlasting light, and the days of thy mourning shall be ended.

66:1-2 Thus saith the LORD, The heaven *is* my throne, and the earth *is* my footstool: where *is* the house that ye build unto me? and where *is* the place of my rest? For all those *things* hath mine hand made, and all those *things* have been, saith the LORD: but to this *man* will I look, *even* to *him that is* poor and of a contrite spirit, and trembleth at my word

Joel

2:28 And it shall come to pass afterward, *that* I will pour out my spirit upon all flesh; and your sons and your daughters shall prophesy, your old men shall dream dreams, your young men shall see visions.

Micah

3:11 The heads thereof judge for reward, and the priests thereof teach for hire, and the prophets thereof divine for money: yet will they lean upon the LORD, and say, *Is* not the LORD among us? none evil can come upon us.

6:8 He hath shewed thee, O man, what is good; and what doth the LORD require of thee, but to do justly, and to love mercy, and to walk humbly with thy God?

Matthew

3:11 I indeed baptize you with water unto repentance: but he that cometh after me is mightier than I, whose shoes I am not worthy to bear: he shall baptize you with the Holy Ghost, and *with* fire.

4:16 The people which sat in darkness saw great light; and to them which sat in the region and shadow of death light is sprung up.

5:14 Ye are the light of the world. A city that is set on an hill cannot be hid.

5:34 But I say unto you, Swear not at all; neither by heaven; for it is God's throne.

5:37 But let your communication be, Yea, yea; Nay, nay: for whatsoever is more than these cometh of evil.

7:23 And then will I profess unto them, I never knew you: depart from me, ye that work iniquity.

7:24-25 Therefore whosoever heareth these sayings of mine, and doeth them, I will liken him unto a wise man, which built his house upon a rock: And the rain descended, and the floods came, and the winds blew, and beat upon that house; and it fell not: for it was founded upon a rock.

7:29 For he taught them as *one* having authority, and not as the scribes.

10:8 Heal the sick, cleanse the lepers, raise the dead, cast out devils: freely ye have received, freely give.

10:19 But when they deliver you up, take no thought how or what ye shall speak: for it shall be given you in that same hour what ye shall speak.

11:29-30 Take my yoke upon you, and learn of me; for I am meek and lowly in heart: and ye shall find rest unto your souls. For my yoke *is* easy, and my burden is light.

13:19 When any one heareth the word of the kingdom, and understandeth *it* not, then cometh the wicked *one*, and catcheth away that which was sown in his heart. This is he which received seed by the way side.

13:23 But he that received seed into the good ground is he that heareth the word, and understandeth *it*; which also beareth fruit, and bringeth forth, some an hundredfold, some sixty, some thirty.

13:33 Another parable spake he unto them; The kingdom of heaven is like unto leaven, which a woman took, and hid in three measures of meal, till the whole was leavened.

25:23 His lord said unto him, Well done, good and faithful servant; thou hast been faithful over a few things, I will make thee ruler over many things: enter thou into the joy of thy lord.

25:34 Then shall the King say unto them on his right hand, Come, ye blessed of my Father, inherit the kingdom prepared for you from the foundation of the world.

25:41 Then shall he say also unto them on the left hand, Depart from me, ye cursed, into everlasting fire, prepared for the devil and his angels.

Mark

3:27 No man can enter into a strong man's house, and spoil his goods, except he will first bind the strong man; and then he will spoil his house.

4:19 And the cares of this world, and the deceitfulness of riches, and the lusts of other things entering in, choke the word, and it becometh unfruitful.

12:38 And he said unto them in his doctrine, Beware of the scribes, which love to go in long clothing, and *love* salutations in the marketplaces.

Luke

1:79 To give light to them that sit in darkness and *in* the shadow of death, to guide our feet into the way of peace.

2:32 A light to lighten the Gentiles, and the glory of thy people Israel.

10:4 Carry neither purse, nor scrip, nor shoes: and salute no man by the way.

12:11 And when they bring you unto the synagogues, and *unto* magistrates, and powers, take ye no thought how or what thing ye shall answer, or what ye shall say.

15:8 Either what woman having ten pieces of silver, if she lose one piece, doth not light a candle, and sweep the house, and seek diligently till she find *it?*

19:20 And another came, saying, Lord, behold, *here is* thy pound, which I have kept laid up in a napkin.

19:23 Wherefore then gavest not thou my money into the bank, that at my coming I might have required mine own with usury?

John

1:1 In the beginning was the Word, and the Word was with God, and the Word was God.

1:3 All things were made by him; and without him was not any thing made that was made.

1:4 In him was life; and the life was the light of men.

1:5 And the light shineth in darkness; and the darkness comprehended it not.

1:6 There was a man sent from God, whose name *was* John.

1:7 There was a man sent from God, whose name *was* John. The same came for a witness, to bear witness of the Light, that all *men* through him might believe.

1:8 He was not that Light, but *was sent* to bear witness of that Light.

1:9 *That* was the true Light, which lighteth every man that cometh into the world.

1:13 Which were born, not of blood, nor of the will of the flesh, nor of the will of man, but of God.

1:14 And the Word was made flesh, and dwelt among us, (and we beheld his glory, the glory as of the only begotten of the Father,) full of grace and truth.

1:16 And of his fulness have all we received, and grace for grace.

1:17 For the law was given by Moses, *but* grace and truth came by Jesus Christ.

1:29 The next day John seeth Jesus coming unto him, and saith, Behold the Lamb of God, which taketh away the sin of the world.

1:33 And I knew him not: but he that sent me to baptize with water, the same said unto me, Upon whom thou shalt see the Spirit descending, and remaining on him, the same is he which baptizeth with the Holy Ghost.

3:5 Jesus answered, Verily, verily, I say unto thee, Except a man be born of water and *of* the Spirit, he cannot enter into the kingdom of God.

3:16 For God so loved the world, that he gave his only begotten Son, that whosoever believeth in him should not perish, but have everlasting life.

3:19 And this is the condemnation, that light is come into the world, and men loved darkness rather than light, because their deeds were evil.

3:20 For every one that doeth evil hateth the light, neither cometh to the light, lest his deeds should be reproved.

3:21 But he that doeth truth cometh to the light, that his deeds may be made manifest, that they are wrought in God.

4:10 Jesus answered and said unto her, If thou knewest the gift of God, and who it is that saith to thee, Give me to drink; thou wouldest have asked of him, and he would have given thee living water.

4:23 But the hour cometh, and now is, when the true worshippers shall worship the Father in spirit and in truth: for the Father seeketh such to worship him.

4:24 God *is* a Spirit: and they that worship him must worship *him* in spirit and in truth.

7:17 If any man will do his will, he shall know of the doctrine, whether it be of God, or *whether* I speak of myself.

8:12 Then spake Jesus again unto them, saying, I am the light of the world: he that followeth me shall not walk in darkness, but shall have the light of life.

8:31 Then said Jesus to those Jews which believed on him, If ye continue in my word, *then* are ye my disciples indeed.

8:46 Which of you convinceth me of sin? And if I say the truth, why do ye not believe me?

10:1-2 Verily, verily, I say unto you, He that entereth not by the door into the sheepfold, but climbeth up some other way, the same is a thief and a robber. But he that entereth in by the door is the shepherd of the sheep.

10:7 Then said Jesus unto them again, Verily, verily, I say unto you, I am the door of the sheep.

12:36 While ye have light, believe in the light, that ye may be the children of light. These things spake Jesus, and departed, and did hide himself from them

14:6 Jesus saith unto him, I am the way, the truth, and the life: no man cometh unto the Father, but by me.

14:15 If ye love me, keep my commandments.

14:17 *Even* the Spirit of truth; whom the world cannot receive, because it seeth him not, neither knoweth him: but ye know him; for he dwelleth with you, and shall be in you.

14:23 Jesus answered and said unto him, If a man love me, he will keep my words: and my Father will love him, and we will come unto him, and make our abode with him.

16:8 And when he is come, he will reprove the world of sin, and of righteousness, and of judgment.

16:13 Howbeit when he, the Spirit of truth, is come, he will guide you into all truth: for he shall not speak of himself; but whatsoever he shall hear, *that* shall he speak: and he will shew you things to come.

17:3 And this is life eternal, that they might know thee the only true God, and Jesus Christ, whom thou hast sent.

17:23 I in them, and thou in me, that they may be made perfect in one; and that the world may know that thou hast sent me, and hast loved them, as thou hast loved me.

Acts

2:17 And it shall come to pass in the last days, saith God, I will pour out of my Spirit upon all flesh: and your sons and your daughters shall prophesy, and your young men shall see visions, and your old men shall dream dreams.

2:47 Praising God, and having favour with all the people. And the Lord added to the church daily such as should be saved.

8:18-20 And when Simon saw that through laying on of the apostles' hands the Holy Ghost was given, he offered them money, Saying, Give me also this power, that on whomsoever I lay hands, he may receive the Holy Ghost. But Peter said unto him, Thy money perish with thee, because thou hast thought that the gift of God may be purchased with money

17:28 For in him we live, and move, and have our being; as certain also of your own poets have said, For we are also his offspring.

26:18 To open their eyes, *and* to turn *them* from darkness to light, and *from* the power of Satan unto God, that they may receive forgiveness of sins, and inheritance among them which are sanctified by faith that is in me.

Romans

1:19 Because that which may be known of God is manifest in them; for God hath shewed *it* unto them.

2:7-9 To them who by patient continuance in well doing seek for glory and honour and immortality, eternal life: But unto them that are contentious, and do not obey the truth, but obey unrighteousness, indignation and wrath, Tribulation and anguish, upon every soul of man that doeth evil, of the Jew first, and also of the Gentile.

2:14-16 For when the Gentiles, which have not the law, do by nature the things contained in the law, these, having not the law, are a law unto themselves: Which shew the work of the law written in their hearts, their conscience also bearing witness, and *their* thoughts the mean while accusing or else excusing one another; In the day when God shall judge the secrets of men by Jesus Christ according to my gospel.

5:6 For when we were yet without strength, in due time Christ died for the ungodly.

6:11 Likewise reckon ye also yourselves to be dead indeed unto sin, but alive unto God through Jesus Christ our Lord.

6:16 Know ye not, that to whom ye yield yourselves servants to obey, his servants ye are to whom ye obey; whether of sin unto death, or of obedience unto righteousness?

8:1 *There is* therefore now no condemnation to them which are in Christ Jesus, who walk not after the flesh, but after the Spirit.

8:9 But ye are not in the flesh, but in the Spirit, if so be that the Spirit of God dwell in you. Now if any man have not the Spirit of Christ, he is none of his.

8:14 For as many as are led by the Spirit of God, they are the sons of God.

8:15 For ye have not received the spirit of bondage again to fear; but ye have received the Spirit of adoption, whereby we cry, Abba, Father.

8:16 The Spirit itself beareth witness with our spirit, that we are the children of God.

10:6-8 But the righteousness which is of faith speaketh on this wise, Say not in thine heart, Who shall ascend into heaven? (that is, to bring Christ down *from above*:) Or, Who shall descend into the deep? (that is, to bring up Christ again from the dead.) But what saith it? The word is nigh thee, *even* in thy mouth, and in thy heart: that is, the word of faith, which we preach.

10:9 That if thou shalt confess with thy mouth the Lord Jesus, and shalt believe in thine heart that God hath raised him from the dead, thou shalt be saved.

12:1 I beseech you therefore, brethren, by the mercies of God, that ye present your bodies a living sacrifice, holy, acceptable unto God, *which is* your reasonable service.

12:2 And be not conformed to this world: but be ye transformed by the renewing of your mind, that ye may prove what *is* that good, and acceptable, and perfect, will of God.

13:12 The night is far spent, the day is at hand: let us therefore cast off the works of darkness, and let us put on the armour of light.

14:5-8 One man esteemeth one day above another: another esteemeth every day *alike*. Let every man be fully persuaded in his own mind. He that regardeth the day, regardeth *it* unto the Lord; and he that regardeth not the day, to the Lord he doth not regard *it*. He that eateth, eateth to the Lord, for he giveth

God thanks; and he that eateth not, to the Lord he eateth not, and giveth God thanks. For none of us liveth to himself, and no man dieth to himself. For whether we live, we live unto the Lord; and whether we die, we die unto the Lord: whether we live therefore, or die, we are the Lord's.

14:17 For the kingdom of God is not meat and drink; but righteousness, and peace, and joy in the Holy Ghost.

First Corinthians

1:3-5 Grace *be* unto you, and peace, from God our Father, and *from* the Lord Jesus Christ. I thank my God always on your behalf, for the grace of God which is given you by Jesus Christ; That in every thing ye are enriched by him, in all utterance, and *in* all knowledge.

1:21 For after that in the wisdom of God the world by wisdom knew not God, it pleased God by the foolishness of preaching to save them that believe.

2:7 But we speak the wisdom of God in a mystery, *even* the hidden *wisdom*, which God ordained before the world unto our glory.

2:10 But God hath revealed *them* unto us by his Spirit: for the Spirit searcheth all things, yea, the deep things of God.

2:11 For what man knoweth the things of a man, save the spirit of man which is in him? even so the things of God knoweth no man, but the Spirit of God.

2:12 Now we have received, not the spirit of the world, but the spirit which is of God; that we might know the things that are freely given to us of God.

2:15 But he that is spiritual judgeth all things, yet he himself is judged of no man.

8:6 But to us *there is but* one God, the Father, of whom *are* all things, and we in him; and one Lord Jesus Christ, by whom *are* all things, and we by him.

12:7 But the manifestation of the Spirit is given to every man to profit withal.

14:3,6,31 But he that prophesieth speaketh unto men *to* edification, and exhortation, and comfort. . . . Now, brethren, if I come unto you speaking with tongues, what shall I profit you, except I shall speak to you either by revelation, or by knowledge, or by prophesying, or by doctrine? . . . For ye may all prophesy one by one, that all may learn, and all may be comforted.

15:45,47 And so it is written, The first man Adam was made a living soul; the last Adam *was made* a quickening spirit. . . . The first man *is* of the earth, earthy: the second man *is* the Lord from heaven.

Second Corinthians

2:11 Lest Satan should get an advantage of us: for we are not ignorant of his devices.

3:18 But we all, with open face beholding as in a glass the glory of the Lord, are changed into the same image from glory to glory, *even* as by the Spirit of the Lord

4:6 For God, who commanded the light to shine out of darkness, hath shined in our hearts, to *give* the light of the knowledge of the glory of God in the face of Jesus Christ.

5:15 And *that* he died for all, that they which live should not henceforth live unto themselves, but unto him which died for them, and rose again.

5:17 Therefore if any man *be* in Christ, *he is* a new creature: old things are passed away; behold, all things are become new.

5:21 For he hath made him *to be* sin for us, who knew no sin; that we might be made the righteousness of God in him.

6:14 Be ye not unequally yoked together with unbelievers: for what fellowship hath righteousness with unrighteousness? and what communion hath light with darkness?

10:3-4 For though we walk in the flesh, we do not war after the flesh: (For the weapons of our warfare *are* not carnal, but mighty through God to the pulling down of strong holds).

12:9 And he said unto me, My grace is sufficient for thee: for my strength is made perfect in weakness. Most gladly therefore will I rather glory in my infirmities, that the power of Christ may rest upon me.

2:15 For we are unto God a sweet savour of Christ, in them that are saved, and in them that perish.

13:5 Examine yourselves, whether ye be in the faith; prove your own selves. Know ye not your own selves, how that Jesus Christ is in you, except ye be reprobates?

Galatians

1:15-16 But when it pleased God, who separated me from my mother's womb, and called *me* by his grace, To reveal his Son in me, that I might preach him among the heathen; immediately I conferred not with flesh and blood.

2:20 I am crucified with Christ: nevertheless I live; yet not I, but Christ liveth in me: and the life which I now live in the flesh I live by the faith of the Son of God, who loved me, and gave himself for me

5:16 This I say then, Walk in the Spirit, and ye shall not fulfil the lust of the flesh.

6:7 Be not deceived; God is not mocked: for whatsoever a man soweth, that shall he also reap.

6:15-16 For in Christ Jesus neither circumcision availeth any thing, nor uncircumcision, but a new creature. And as many as walk according to this rule, peace *be* on them, and mercy, and upon the Israel of God.

Ephesians

4:7 But unto every one of us is given grace according to the measure of the gift of Christ.

4:8 Wherefore he saith, When he ascended up on high, he led captivity captive, and gave gifts unto men.

5:8 For ye were sometimes darkness, but now *are ye* light in the Lord: walk as children of light.

5:13 But all things that are reproved are made manifest by the light: for whatsoever doth make manifest is light.

5:15 See then that ye walk circumspectly, not as fools, but as wise.

6:16 Above all, taking the shield of faith, wherewith ye shall be able to quench all the fiery darts of the wicked.

6:17 And take the helmet of salvation, and the sword of the Spirit, which is the word of God.

Philippians

1:21 For to me to live *is* Christ, and to die *is* gain.

2:12 Wherefore, my beloved, as ye have always obeyed, not as in my presence only, but now much more in my absence, work out your own salvation with fear and trembling.

3:10 That I may know him, and the power of his resurrection, and the fellowship of his sufferings, being made conformable unto his death.

4:5 Let your moderation be known unto all men. The Lord *is* at hand.

Colossians

1:12 Giving thanks unto the Father, which hath made us meet to be partakers of the inheritance of the saints in light.

1:13 Who hath delivered us from the power of darkness, and hath translated *us* into the kingdom of his dear Son.

1:26-27 *Even* the mystery which hath been hid from ages and from generations, but now is made manifest to his saints: To whom God would make known what *is* the riches of the glory of this mystery among the Gentiles; which is Christ in you, the hope of glory.

2:16-17 Let no man therefore judge you in meat, or in drink, or in respect of an holyday, or of the new moon, or of the sabbath *days*: Which are a shadow of things to come; but the body *is* of Christ.

First Thessalonians

4:9 But as touching brotherly love ye need not that I write unto you: for ye yourselves are taught of God to love one another.

5:4 But ye, brethren, are not in darkness, that that day should overtake you as a thief.

5:5 Ye are all the children of light, and the children of the day: we are not of the night, nor of darkness.

First Timothy

2:4 Who will have all men to be saved, and to come unto the knowledge of the truth.

6:12 Fight the good fight of faith, lay hold on eternal life, whereunto thou art also called, and hast professed a good profession before many witnesses.

6:16 Who only hath immortality, dwelling in the light which no man can approach unto; whom no man hath seen, nor can see: to whom *be* honour and power everlasting. Amen.

Titus

2:11-12 For the grace of God that bringeth salvation hath appeared to all men, Teaching us that, denying ungodliness and worldly lusts, we should live soberly, righteously, and godly, in this present world

2:13 Looking for that blessed hope, and the glorious appearing of the great God and our Saviour Jesus Christ.

3:4 But after that the kindness and love of God our Saviour toward man appeared.

Hebrews

2:17 Wherefore in all things it behoved him to be made like unto *his* brethren, that he might be a merciful and faithful high priest in things *pertaining* to God, to make reconciliation for the sins of the people.

3:1 Wherefore, holy brethren, partakers of the heavenly calling, consider the Apostle and High Priest of our profession, Christ Jesus.

4:15 For we have not an high priest which cannot be touched with the feeling of our infirmities; but was in all points tempted like as *we are, yet* without sin.

5:8 Though he were a Son, yet learned he obedience by the things which he suffered.

6:15 And so, after he had patiently endured, he obtained the promise.

10:10 By the which will we are sanctified through the offering of the body of Jesus Christ once *for all.*

10:20 By a new and living way, which he hath consecrated for us, through the veil, that is to say, his flesh.

10:25 Not forsaking the assembling of ourselves together, as the manner of some *is*; but exhorting *one another*: and so much the more, as ye see the day approaching.

12:9 Furthermore we have had fathers of our flesh which corrected *us*, and we gave *them* reverence: shall we not much rather be in subjection unto the Father of spirits, and live?

James

1:17 Every good gift and every perfect gift is from above, and cometh down from the Father of lights, with whom is no variableness, neither shadow of turning.

5:12 But above all things, my brethren, swear not, neither by heaven, neither by the earth, neither by any other oath: but let your yea be yea; and *your* nay, nay; lest ye fall into condemnation.

First Peter

1:23 Being born again, not of corruptible seed, but of incorruptible, by the word of God, which liveth and abideth for ever.

2:9 But ye *are* a chosen generation, a royal priesthood, an holy nation, a peculiar people; that ye should shew forth the praises of him who hath called you out of darkness into his marvellous light.

2:24 Who his own self bare our sins in his own body on the tree, that we, being dead to sins, should live unto righteousness: by whose stripes ye were healed.

4:11 If any man speak, *let him speak* as the oracles of God; if any man minister, *let him do it* as of the ability which God giveth: that God in all things may be glorified through Jesus Christ, to whom be praise and dominion for ever and ever. Amen.

Second Peter

1:4 Whereby are given unto us exceeding great and precious promises: that by these ye might be partakers of the divine nature, having escaped the corruption that is in the world through lust.

1:10 Wherefore the rather, brethren, give diligence to make your calling and election sure: for if ye do these things, ye shall never fall.

3:13 Nevertheless we, according to his promise, look for new heavens and a new earth, wherein dwelleth righteousness.

First John

1:1 That which was from the beginning, which we have heard, which we have seen with our eyes, which we have looked upon, and our hands have handled, of the Word of life.

1:3 That which we have seen and heard declare we unto you, that ye also may have fellowship with us: and truly our fellowship *is* with the Father, and with his Son Jesus Christ.

1:5 This then is the message which we have heard of him, and declare unto you, that God is light, and in him is no darkness at all.

1:6 If we say that we have fellowship with him, and walk in darkness, we lie, and do not the truth.

1:7 But if we walk in the light, as he is in the light, we have fellowship one with another, and the blood of Jesus Christ his Son cleanseth us from all sin.

2:8 Again, a new commandment I write unto you, which thing is true in him and in you: because the darkness is past, and the true light now shineth.

2:9 He that saith he is in the light, and hateth his brother, is in darkness even until now.

2:20 But ye have an unction from the Holy One, and ye know all things.

2:26 These *things* have I written unto you concerning them that seduce you.

2:27 But the anointing which ye have received of him abideth in you, and ye need not that any man teach you: but as the same anointing teacheth you of all things, and is truth, and is no lie, and even as it hath taught you, ye shall abide in him.

3:7 Little children, let no man deceive you: he that doeth righteousness is righteous, even as he is righteous.

3:9 Whosoever is born of God doth not commit sin; for his seed remaineth in him: and he cannot sin, because he is born of God.

3:20-21 For if our heart condemn us, God is greater than our heart, and knoweth all things. Beloved, if our heart condemn us not, *then* have we confidence toward God.

5:10 He that believeth on the Son of God hath the witness in himself: he that believeth not God hath made him a liar; because he believeth not the record that God gave of his Son.

5:12 He that hath the Son hath life; *and* he that hath not the Son of God hath not life.

Third John

1:11 Beloved, follow not that which is evil, but that which is good. He that doeth good is of God: but he that doeth evil hath not seen God.

Revelation

3:7 And to the angel of the church in Philadelphia write; These things saith he that is holy, he that is true, he that hath the key of David, he that openeth, and no man shutteth; and shutteth, and no man openeth.

3:20 Behold, I stand at the door, and knock: if any man hear my voice, and open the door, I will come in to him, and will sup with him, and he with me.

21:5 And he that sat upon the throne said, Behold, I make all things new. And he said unto me, Write: for these words are true and faithful.

21:22 And I saw no temple therein: for the Lord God Almighty and the Lamb are the temple of it.

21:23-24 And the city had no need of the sun, neither of the moon, to shine in it: for the glory of God did lighten it, and the Lamb *is* the light thereof. And the nations of them which are saved shall walk in the light of it: and the kings of the earth do bring their glory and honour into it.

22:5 And there shall be no night there; and they need no candle, neither light of the sun; for the Lord God giveth them light: and they shall reign for ever and ever.

Also available from Inner Light Books

Primitive Quakerism Revived
by Paul Buckley.

ISBN 978-0-9998332-2-3 (hardcover) $25
ISBN 978-0-9998332-3-0 (paperback)$15

Jesus, Christ and Servant of God
Meditations on the Gospel According to John
By David Johnson

ISBN 978–0–9970604–6–1 (hardcover) $35
ISBN 978–0–9970604–7–8 (paperback) $25
ISBN 978–0–9970604–8–5 (eBook) $12.50

The Anti-War
By Douglas Gwyn

ISBN 978-0-9970604-3-0, (hardcover) $30
ISBN 978-0-9970604-4-7, (paperback) $17.50
ISBN 978-0-9970604-5-4, (eBook) $10

Our Life Is Love, the Quaker Spiritual Journey
By Marcelle Martin

ISBN 978-0-9970604-0-9, (hardcover) $30
ISBN 978-0-9970604-1-6, (paperback) $17.50
ISBN 978-0-9970604-2-5, (eBook) $10

A Quaker Prayer Life
By David Johnson

ISBN 978-0-9834980-5-6 (hardcover) $20
ISBN 978-0-9834980-6-3 (paperback) $12.50
ISBN 978-0-9834980-7-0 (eBook) $10

The Essential Elias Hicks
By Paul Buckley

ISBN 978-0-9834980-8-7 (hardcover) $25
ISBN 978-0-9834980-9-4 (paperback) $15

The Journal of Elias Hicks
Edited by Paul Buckley

ISBN 978-0-9797110-4-6, (hardcover) $50
ISBN 978-0-9797110-5-3, (paperback) $30

Dear Friend: The Letters and Essays of Elias Hicks
Edited by Paul Buckley

ISBN 978-0-9834980-0-1 (hardcover) $45
ISBN 978-0-9834980-1-8 (paperback) $25

The Early Quakers and 'the Kingdom of God'
By Gerard Guiton

ISBN 978-0-9834980-2-5, (hardcover) $45
ISBN 978-0-9834980-3-2, (paperback) $25
ISBN 978-0-9834980-4-9, (eBook) $12.50

John Woolman and the Affairs of Truth
Edited by James Proud

ISBN 978-0-9797110-6-0, (hardcover) $45
ISBN 978-0-9797110-7-7, (paperback) $25

Cousin Ann's Stories for Children by Ann Preston
Edited by Richard Beards
Illustrated by Stevie French

ISBN 978-0-9797110-8-4, (hardcover) $20
ISBN 978-0-9797110-9-1, (paperback) $12

Counsel to the Christian-Traveller: also Meditations and Experiences
By William Shewen

ISBN 978-0-9797110-0-8 (hardcover) $25
ISBN 978-0-9797110-1-5 (paperback) $15

CPSIA information can be obtained
at www.ICGtesting.com
Printed in the USA
BVHW030508041218
534640BV00004B/254/P

9 780999 833216